The Dawn Of Life:
SuperNova Innings

AF080780

Sumita

BLUEROSE PUBLISHERS
India | U.K.

Copyright © Sumita 2023

All rights reserved by the author. No part of this publication may be reproduced, stored in a retrieval system or transmitted in any form or by any means, electronic, mechanical, photocopying, recording or otherwise, without the prior permission of the author. Although every precaution has been taken to verify the accuracy of the information contained herein, the publisher assumes no responsibility for any errors or omissions. No liability is assumed for damages that may result from the use of information contained within.

BlueRose Publishers takes no responsibility for any damages, losses, or liabilities that may arise from the use or misuse of the information, products, or services provided in this publication.

For permissions requests or inquiries regarding this publication,
please contact:

BLUEROSE PUBLISHERS
www.BlueRoseONE.com
info@bluerosepublishers.com
+91 8882 898 898
+4407342408967

ISBN: 978-93-5819-179-0

Cover design: Muskan Sachdeva
Typesetting: Namrata Saini

First Edition: November 2023

From Author's Desk

There is a saying that "age is just a number", and I whole-heartedly believe in it.

After completing 50 rounds around the Sun, I suddenly had a new zeal towards life and developed a passion for writing, poetry, painting, video editing and travelling. All these mindful activities fascinated me so much that I started undertaking these endeavours with great jest and eagerness with a silent wish to unfold them before the world. This is the beginning of my book **"The Dawn of Life - Supernova Innings"**.

I started with small write-ups of some of the incidents from my childhood and day-to-day life that left indelible imprints on my mind. While translating these experiences into words, I wondered if it is just a fleeting bout of passion or a way to regain the power to be the author as well as the narrator of my life. But as I wrote some unforgettable memories of my Maa, Baba, Kaku (father's younger brother) and Kaki (Kaku's wife), I realised this is not just an activity for me, but a journey into self-discovery and memorialising the people who had the deepest impact in my life.

Going back in time, my childhood was spent in a family of five children, of which I was the youngest. I grew up pampered by Baba for all things big and small. It is insufficient to say that I was very close to him. When in fact, he was my safe comfortable space in the whole wide universe. So, after his untimely demise in 1984, I became very lonely and quiet. All my siblings are older to me and I was not open to anyone else except my younger cousin Monu. After that slowly, I became close to Maa and was able to pour my heart out to her. But in 2021, my Maa also left us and accompanied Baba. It was the saddest part of my life as I thought I had lost my anchor.

In the beginning of 2019, I shifted to Ghaziabad in my own flat to live all by myself, after separating from my husband. My daughter, Diya

(Deboleena) stayed separately in Delhi where I visited often to spend time with her. I call her place my holiday home. She is my all-time supporter and my backbone. Everyone else was asking me how I could live there all alone. Honestly speaking, I found myself while staying in my flat with my own thoughts to accompany me.

I learnt to recreate my passions in different fields and enjoy every moment of life. The process of aging has definitely improved in my life and I started enjoying my second childhood named **"The Dawn of Life - Supernova Innings"**.

Love

Sumita

About Author by a Spiritual Lady

Hi

I am Sumita,

I know life is not always fantasy but I know how to live up to it.

I have seen ups and downs, but I have learnt to count ups and learn from downs...

I believe much in love and thus I love my family & friends and my hearts mother and daughter, in whom probably you might find a bit of me...

but

I never hold on and now one of my hearts is ready to brighten the society,

"दीया जो है, रोशनी तो फेलाना ही है उसे"

(Diya - The lamp which is there, the light has to be spread from it)

I am life, so I don't wait to celebrate,

when I wanna fly high, I look up and take pictures,

when I remember my childhood I don't regret,

I just become childlike and enjoy...

I am life,

I don't limit myself,

I dance,

I sing,

I recite poem,

I paint,

I do all the activities that need my involvement, because life all about involvement,

lots of people are surviving in this world but I am not satisfied in surviving,

I want to live life.

I don't wait for happiness to knock my door,

I have moulded my heart in a way to create it for all.

I am life and

I appreciate all the colours of life...

Written by

Radha Kar

21.04.21(2021)

*Diya – my daughter's nick name

*My book is dedicated to my beloved
Maa (Late Smt. Anima Dasgupta) and
my beloved Baba (Late Shri Iresh Chandra Dasgupta).*

My daughter Advocate Deboleena Dutta has inspired me to explore new avenues.

Preface

This book is divided into four parts.

The first part of this book is a collection of anecdotal pieces from my memory that have had a significant impact on my life. It is important to note that some of these stories are more than 60 years old and they continue to serve as valuable lessons for us today and for our future generation too.

The second part of this book focuses on the feelings and emotions that I experienced from time to time, and I have written them all down in the form of poetry. Throughout this section, you will find poetry written in three different languages - English, Bengali, and Hindi.

My third contribution on this book showcases the colour of life as and when it entered my mind. I simply took some colours and began painting on canvas. There is nothing real about it, it is all an imagination.

In the fourth part of this book, I have shared my experiences from my first short solo trip. The event came about so spontaneously and was full of fun and excitement. And ended up with lots of memories and pictures.

In writing this book, I poured my heart into each page.

Hope you will enjoy it while going through all of these parts.

Contents

Part 1

Anecdotes   **1**
- a) A Wonderful Couple   3
- b) The Chair   5
- c) Sing Along Ride   8
- d) Metro Art   10
- e) Ice-cream brings happiness   12
- f) The Hero of our family   14
- g) Our beloved Kaki   16
- h) An age-old interview.   18
- i) A day before her last breath   21
- j) *Pages from old memories*   23

Part 2

Rhyme   **31**
1. Little Heart   33
2. I have no regrets in my life   34
3. I am rich, I won't cry   35
4. Life   36
5. Time is flying   37
6. "Maa"   38
7. Last words from a person on death bed   41
8. Choose a caption   42

কবিতা ও গান   **43**
১. আমার বিশ্বাস (Trust between you and me)   45
২. ভালোবাসার গান (A love song)   46
৩. মা ও সন্তান (Deep relation between mother & child)   47
৪. অণু (An explanation of an Atom in real life)   48

शायरी		**49**
१.	ज़िंदगी की तलाश (In search of life)	51
२.	माँ, तू तो माँ है (Our world is complete with you, ma)	52
३.	हमने देखी है दुनिया, बदलते हुए (We have witnessed the changes in the world)	54
४.	अधूरा सपना (Unfulfilled dream)	59
५.	झूठा ख़्वाब (False dream)	60
६.	ज़िन्दगी है (Different version of life)	61
७.	आप, इंसान हो, मेरे दोस्त (A businessman of life is not, what you are)	62
८.	एक मुसाफ़िर (Life is a pleasant journey)	63
९.	सन्नाटा और खामोशी (Love talk between calm & silence)	64
१०.	एक नई सुबह (A new morning)	66
११.	नया दिन (New day)	67
१२.	नन्हे फ़रिस्ते (An angel's life from conception to death)	68
१३.	तस्वीर (Time picture)	69
१४.	यह सफ़र (A sweet journey)	70
१५.	पचपन और बचपन (Combination of age and childhood)	71
१६.	मिलते थे हमें भी ख़त (We used to get letter)	72
१७.	सफल करो सपना (Fullfilled your dream)	74
१८.	तन्हा एक सोच है (Loneliness is a thought only)	75
१९.	ऐसे दर्द भी है (Feeling of pain)	76
२०.	मेरी परछाई (I hear my shadow whispering to me)	77
२१.	सिंपल लाइफ (I would appreciate it if someone could transport me back to those childhood days where life was so simple)	78
२२.	एक कहानी (Life is a novel)	82
२३.	ख़ुशी क्या है? (What is happiness)	83
२४.	कल मैं समा गया आज (Today is lost in time)	87

Part 3

Fun with Colours in Canvas	**89**
1. A lonely Bird	91
2. Carona Mahakal	92
3. Rays of Hope	93
4. Snow Storm	94
5. Night View of Blossom	95
6. Mother's womb	96
7. Feel light like feather	97
8. Where to fly, dark on both sides	98
9. Night view of Niagara Falls in my colours	99
10. A rear piece of old carpet	100
11. Arial view of scattered flowers	101
12. Blurred City view	102
13. Valley of Flowers	103
14. Giant Honeycomb	104
15. Dancing Fountains (inside a cave)	105
16. Happy Hill	106
17. Colour Blast	107
18. Space view from my lens	108
19. Arrival of Spring	109
20. Deadly Storm	110
21. Falling Feathers	111
22. Milky WaterFalls	112
23. Marble on canvas	113

Part 4

My first solo trip	**115**
Some more glimpses of my solo trip	**161**

Part 1

Anecdotes

a) A Wonderful Couple

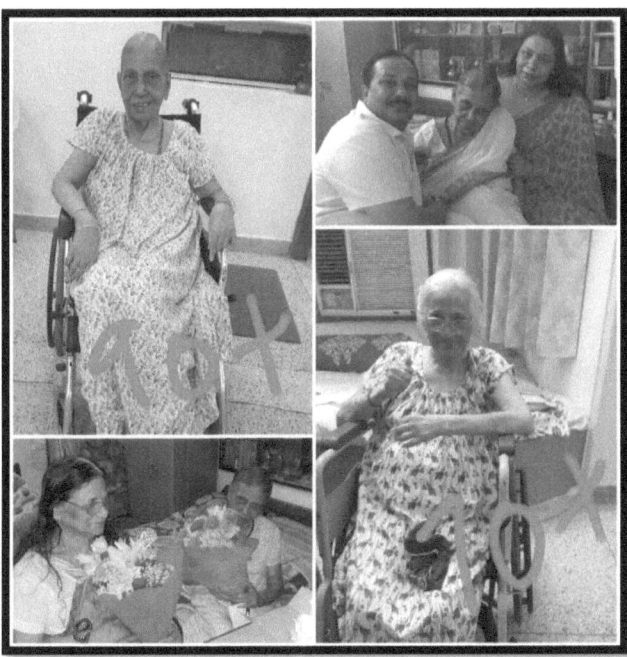

It is natural to experience ups and downs in life, as well as challenges. In order to overcome such challenges, one must remain calm while at the same time being strong enough to face them.

In this article, I am attempting to demonstrate how a gentle couple can cope with these situations and handle all challenges with dignity.

This is a unique yet real story that happened 2 years ago.

I am truly touched by the beautiful bond shared by this wonderful couple, Debu and Shilpi, with their mothers. It is heartwarming to see how a daughter-in-law can become a daughter and a son-in-law can become a son through the love and care they received from both their mothers.

It is truly remarkable that despite the changes and challenges of life, Debu and Shilpi had taken on the responsibility of caring for their mothers, who were in their 90s and 70s. It is evident that they provided constant support and tremendous care for both mothers, creating a loving and nurturing environment in their home.

As a sister, I am grateful to this beautiful couple, especially Shilpi, for taking care of my mother with such grace. It is a testament to their love and dedication. Even as a daughter, I was unable to fully care for my own mother whereas Debu and Shilpi stepped in to fill that role. It will not be possible to accomplish this without the support of Shibu and Rumpa. This is a testament to their selflessness and their commitment to family.

It is beautiful to see how this entire family comes together to devote themselves to their loved ones.

I salute these gentle couples for setting an example for this generation. They have never given up and always kept their heads held high. Despite the hardships, they have taught us that no matter how hard things get, one should never give up. They serve as a great inspiration for all of us and also, they show us that old age is not a reason to be sent to an old home, but rather a time when our loved ones need even more affection. It is through their devotion that they demonstrate the true meaning of family and the importance of nurturing relationships.

May their actions continue to inspire others and may they be blessed with happiness, health, and abundance.

But now, it is hard to believe that both mothers passed away 6 months apart in 2021. It was a difficult time for the family as they had to cope with the loss of their mothers in such a short span of time. They found solace in their strong bond and the support of their friends and family.

I remember both mothers fondly as always smiling and kind to everyone around them. They will be missed by many.

b) The Chair

Despite having a busy schedule, many of us find time in the morning for some exercise or to go for a stroll. It helps to clear the mind and get the day started on a positive note.

I find it's a great way to start the day, the fresh air and the peaceful environment help me to clear my thoughts. I love to take my time to observe my surroundings. I pay attention to the small details, like the lively birds chirping in the trees, the fresh smell of the morning dew, the sun shining through the clouds, etc. The fresh air invigorated my body and I took a deep breath of the cool morning air. It helps me set my intentions for the day and feel more energized.

My experience during a morning walk at Diya's Malviya Nagar house prompted me to write this.

Prior to my surgery, I walked in a park near her house around 9 am. After walking around a park, I took a road towards the Gurdwara.

While passing through the Gurdwara, I saw an old man sitting on a chair on the opposite side of the Gurdwara. Throughout the street, I noticed that he waved his hand at passersby and handed out something from his pocket, the one who was near to him. In the same way, he also called me. But I felt very uncomfortable, so I walked away. After I left the place, I thought about that incident and looked back to see the old man.

After a while, a woman in a saree approached him from the opposite side of the road and touched his feet. I paused and watched what was taking place. The old man gave her something from his pocket. She took it as prasad and touched his feet again before leaving the place. I was wondering what he gave to that lady and she was so pleased to have those things.

Even though I left the place, I promised myself that I would visit him tomorrow morning.

As I woke up the next day, I recalled the incident from the previous day near the Gurdwara.

During my regular morning walk around the same time, I walked up to him and was delighted to see him. As I greeted him, he gave me his blessings along with these toffees and dry fruits. My surprise at receiving such a kind gesture from an elderly man was overwhelming.

After a few seconds, I left the place so overwhelmed that on the way back I decided to take his interview the following day.

After reaching the location the next morning, I was unable to find him. I was there for quite a while but the old man did not come. I took a photo of his chair because I thought the old man did not come every day. Despite my diligent efforts, I could not find anyone to inquire about his whereabouts.

For me this incident always remains an incomplete story in my memory as I could not record that old man's life journey.

Moral: We should respect old people's love and at the same time we should love them more.

My morning walk experience was published in "The Statesman" on May 30, 2022.

c) Sing Along Ride

In Delhi, Auto ride is the most comfortable, fast, efficient and cost-effective transport solution when there is a shortage of public transportation.

Additionally, it is the fastest and most reliable option if you don't own a car. They provide customers with a convenient way to get to their destination.

It is often troublesome to get home late at night if you do not have a safe means of transport. This is especially true for all working women who do not have their own conveyance. They too need to be concerned about their personal safety when using public transport.

Moreover, cab and auto drivers usually charge a hefty amount even for a short ride during crises.

Here I am sharing an auto ride experience that happened to me on 25th February 2020 when I was returning home from work at night.

There was neither a cab nor an auto available and the one that was available charged a hefty amount.

Moreover, the demand for Ola and Uber services was high. After 15/20 minutes of desperate waiting, I flagged down a passing auto and met 5 other female passengers who were luckily going in the same direction as me.

Although the driver asked for a large amount of money, I decided to get into the vehicle as we had to divide the money among 6 people. All the seats were occupied by the other women except the seat next to the driver. As I could not find any other alternative, I had to take the seat next to the driver.

The first time I sat next to the driver, I felt like a hero from a Hindi film.

My co-passengers were all professional women between the ages of 24 and 30. Two of them were married. And I was the oldest of them.

Soon after we left, the driver turned on the radio, but I told him to turn it off and since we were all women, we would sing our own songs. I started and soon others joined in. Everyone enjoyed the variety of songs, even the driver sang a few songs when he felt like it.

All in all, it was a beautiful, unforgettable evening for all of us. The one-hour drive flew by and we felt very refreshed and in good spirits. An auto ride finally became a joyful experience.

The moral of this experience is that we can find happiness anywhere if we only look for it.

My auto ride experience was published in the newspaper "The Statesman" on 23 March 2020.

The Statesman Mon, 23 March 2020
https://epaper.thestatesman.

d) Metro Art

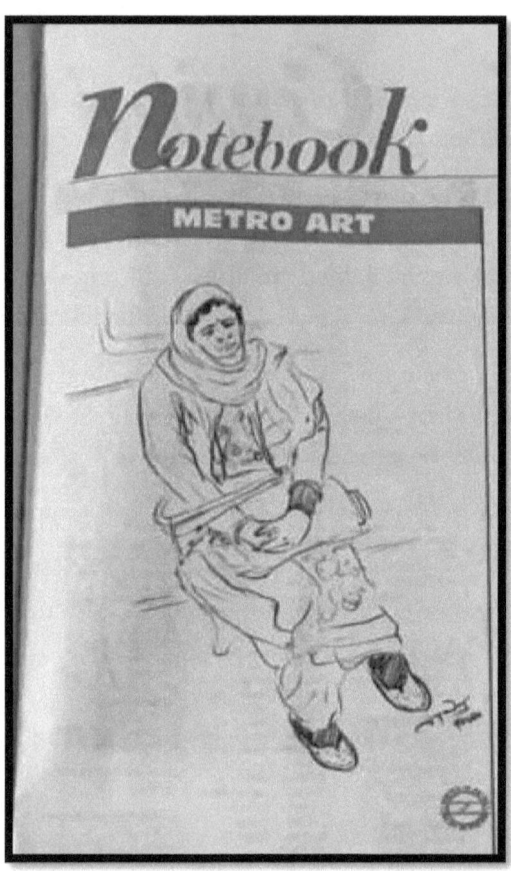

I would like to share an interesting experience during peak traffic hour on the Metro. There are times when unwanted attention, especially from a stranger, can be a big surprise during a metro ride.

March 11, 2020 was like any other busy day for me and I waited for the metro on my way home from work. While traveling from Green Park to Rajiv Chowk, I contemplated my own thoughts. This is every day and the 15-minute journey becomes routine.

But it was no ordinary day, when I noticed a young man in a turban, a Sikh, staring at me all the time. I had my eyes closed most of the time, but every single time I opened my eyes, I noticed that this young man was staring at me and watching me very closely.

I knew something was going on, but later realized that he was sketching me on his device. He showed it to me once he completed it. He told me that he was an architect and had recently started sketching every day on the metro.

He usually travels during rush hour, so he stands at a convenient spot with his iPad and pen to artistically capture what he sees.

The suggestion I made to him was to print these sketches and make a folio. He plans to do so when 1000 of these are made. He has finished only 50 sketches so far but there are still a lot of sketches to go.

This is the day made special for me by another stranger, Gagan. His creativity, love and passion for art were truly inspiring and made me realize that there is still beauty to be found in this world. It was an experience I will never forget.

Having seen his artwork, I was willing to publish it.

I received this response from him after telling him that I'd like to publish this metro experience.

On 16th March 2020, it appeared in the newspaper "The Statesman".

e) Ice-cream brings happiness

The joy of ice cream can be felt by all.

The following story is about my Maa (97 yrs. Old lady) during her illness when she was not eating properly, and how an ice cream brought her happiness during that time.

I visited Maa's residence on 08.03.2021 at C.R.Park, New Delhi. She seemed very dull and showed no interest in food or TV shows and was not excited about meeting people. Ofcourse, she smiled at everyone who came to see her.

Then something strange happened.

She exhibited no interest when I requested tea or coffee or fruit around 5pm, but when I inquired (out of curiosity) about mango duet (her favourite ice cream), she nodded her head. It prompted me to ask Shilpi (my sister-in-law who cares for Maa) if I could get it for her.

Shilpi also said, "yes, you can, but just a little bit".

It was great to see her so happy. After a few bites, I said enough, but she looked at the plate and saw that there was still some ice cream left, so she wanted to have more and continued to look at it until it had finished.

It was a stressful time for me too, so I asked Shilpi again if I should give her more. Shilpi said to me that let her enjoy the ice cream and she would give Maa some medicine at night to maintain her health.

Giving her some happiness at this age was an amazing experience - something she might not be able to reveal to anyone, but it was her wish to have her favourite ice cream.

In addition to glowing, she looked better after eating ice cream.

"Ice-cream brings happiness" - it is not only a saying but actually brings happiness to all ages.

You may also try it if you are feeling low.

These lines popped into my head when I saw the happy face of my Maa after having ice cream.

Ice-cream

*Oh! my love,
ice-cream,
You are always melting sweet.*

*As soon as I taste your sweetness,
I am filled with a sense of magical happiness.*

*Whether you are flavoured in candy or cream,
Your texture does not matter to me.*

*Whether you are hard or soft,
Your sweetness makes me happy even more.*

*Whether you are in a cup or on a stick,
The more I lick, the more I enjoy it.*

*Whether I am a young or an old,
Every time I see you,
I feel again I am a child of three-year-old.*

*I find that every bite I take
has an element of bliss
hidden within it,
regardless of whether I am healthy or sick.*

f) The Hero of our family

I am writing about the true story of a young boy from Bangladesh who came to India (before partition) to achieve his life's goal.

My Kaku (father's younger brother) is Late Shri Srish Chandra Dasgupta (popularly known as S.C. Dasgupta) of Moti Bagh, New Delhi.

A little boy of Moulvibazar, Gharua, Bangladesh, who had a dream to settle in New Delhi and study up to Post graduation.

On 30th June 1948, he travelled from Kolkata to Delhi by Toofan Mail paying Rs 9 for the ticket to fulfil all his dreams. He achieved his dreams and became a post graduate govt. Employee living in Moti Bagh, New Delhi.

In fact, he has a double master degree in History and English.

But that was not enough.

Thereafter, he took upon a challenge to open a Bengali School in his area. He struggled for many years and eventually opened **Bidhan Chandra Vidyalaya**, established on 1st July 1962 and named after great doctor and Bharat Ratna Dr. Bidhan Chandra Roy.

He became the Secretary of the school committee for many years.

Initially it was up to class VIII with not more than fifty students on roll. Now it is a senior secondary school with more than thousand students with all 3 streams Arts, Commerce and Science.

But this was only the beginning.

Being a deeply cultural man, he went on to bring Bengali tradition and festivals to Moti Bagh. He became the Secretary of Durga Puja Moti Bagh committee and organised Durga Puja for many years.

In those days, the most popular Bengali cultural program was jatra, and he also became a member of **Sreemoti Opera Jatra** dol.

Since he hailed from Sylhet and in those days very few of them were in Delhi, so they thought of meeting with families from the origin and decided to have picnics at least once in a year. And then they formed **Srihotto Sammelani**.

He always aimed to be rich in culture and education, and he did both. He also fulfilled his dream of having a bungalow of his own.

Yes, he did it all.

My pranam to Kaku wherever you are.

g) Our beloved Kaki

The true story of a courageous lady who survived in a male-oriented environment. She is none other than my kaki (Kaku's wife) Late Shrimati Bela Rani Dasgupta.

It was in the early 60s. She got married and came from Hailakandi (Assam) to New Delhi. She started her career in the Indian Post Office in Hailakandi and after her marriage she took transfer to Moti Bagh branch, New Delhi. My Kaku, who too was in Government service, got a Government flat there.

She was very courageous, fearless and always cared for family members which was an example set for us. She was the perfect life partner for our Kaku.

The Moti Bagh branch post office is situated at Basrurkar Market, Moti Bagh, New Delhi.

When she joined that branch, she was a very young, beautiful, newly married lady and the only female in that branch.

Due to the fact that the area was a market, and most of the people around her were men, she was very strict with the way she handled her job and communicated.

All market owners, shopkeepers, workers and people around the market addressed her as Bela ji and had great respect for her.

She was also a very dedicated member in Durga puja, Moti Bagh. She was always busy in puja mandap during Durga puja and Kali puja.

The best part of her life was that she spent most of her working life in Moti Bagh post office and retired from the same branch as postmaster after serving more than 30 years in Indian Postal service.

During her service she got transferred 3 times but after a few months of servicing in different branches, she came back again to Moti Bagh branch.

After retirement a few years back, my cousin (her daughter) Monu took her to her branch post office and visited different shops in that market.

Many things and people have changed.

The famous sweet shop Sheetal, still exists with a new ambience. When they entered that sweet shop, one of the old men recognized her and with great respect welcomed her to the shop.

She was so happy to know that people still recognized her.

Her life journey was a lesson for us.

"If you are mentally strong, you can handle all difficulties in your life."

h) An age-old interview.

There was a time when marriages were arranged by the elders of both families. There was no culture of meeting the bride and groom before the wedding. The elders decided regarding the bride and groom. It was the elders who selected a bride for the groom and the other way around.

In the years following independence, Bangladesh was a part of India, and this is the story of a lady from Bangladesh.

When she was nine years old, she lost her mother, and she also had a brother who was five years old. She witnessed all the war trauma and was a witness to partition.

We all know through our fairy tale stories that step mothers were not an ideal lady nor kind hearted, always discriminating between her own child and step child. However, here the situation was completely different.

After her father's second marriage, she gained a mother (a stepmother, as usual) and later three more sisters and two brothers. They all grew up together and there was a healthy relationship between them. All the kids loved her and they gradually loved her more and more. She was the favourite Didi for all kids.

Moving forward, the time came for her marriage.

Three gentlemen came to her for a marriage interview. They came from a highly educated family; they were called pandits (not by surname but by their teaching profession).

In those days, it was common for the prospective bride to receive questions from elders, and she had to impress them with her answer, and presence of mind.

The first gentleman asked her, "Which is the pulse (daal) boiling fast?".

Her answer was Moong daal.

The second gentleman asked her, "If you had given one rupee to distribute among two in such a way that one should get one Aana more than the other".

(That was the time when Anna was an Indian local trader. 1 rupee is equal to 16 aana)

The answers she provided were 7.5 and 8.5 respectively.

The third gentleman then asked, "If there is a scarcity of food, how will you sustain your household?"

In response, she stated, "I will not experience such a situation at home as I will store a small amount of food every day in my stock and I will use it if the need arises."

Again, the same gentleman asked her, "how will you feed some guests if they suddenly appear at your house at lunchtime, without waiting and without sharing your meal?"

In response to this question, she explained, "If any guest comes to my home during lunch or dinner time, I can easily feed them without sharing my own meal since I always cook more so that all of my guests can enjoy the same meal as I do."

The three gentlemen were delighted to receive such beautiful responses.

Finally, she became the bride of that pandits family and moved directly from Bangladesh to New Delhi, India.

She is none other than my beloved Maa.

She was always ready to welcome her guests with open arms and a warm meal. Her hospitality and generosity know no bounds. She had left a feeling of warmth and love in many of us.

Today, in her absence, the same practice continues at her house. Any guest appearing at any time may enjoy the meal at her home. Her teachings about life have been invaluable to us and we are striving to follow the path she paved for us.

The love of my mother will always remain in my heart.

i) A day before her last breath

Maa was in bed before her last breath 17.8.2021, 3:55am.

I was sitting next to Maa, a day before her last breath.

She showed all the facial expressions one can have, a day before her last breath.

I have seen her laughing with full of joy, a day before her last breath.

And in the next minute, I saw her crying as if some close one was departing from her, a day before her last breath.

I have seen her open eyes but she was neither looking at me nor anyone else in the room, a day before her last breath.

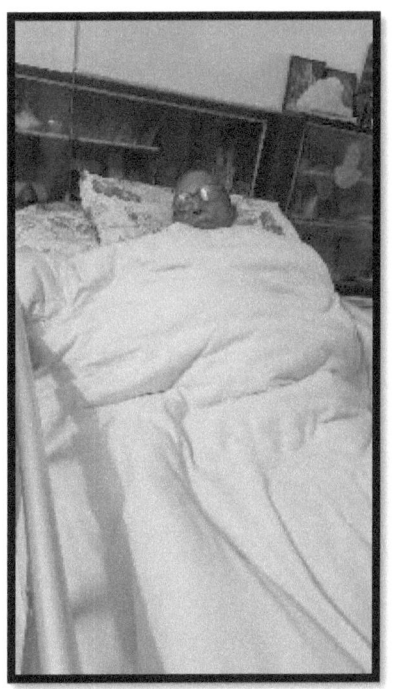

I have seen her looking up at the ceiling as if she was watching her life journey, a day before her last breath.

I have seen her tears rolling down her cheek from her eyes as if she was going through a lot of pain, a day before her last breath.

I have seen her anger as if some wrong thing was happening around, a day before her last breath.

I could feel the touch of my Maa but she was not responding to my touch, a day before her last breath.

She was in between life and death, a day before her last breath.

She was in between earth and universe, a day before her last breath.

She was detaching herself from all connections of this life, a day before her last breath.

Maa o Maa, I am attached to you forever.

Love you and will miss you always till my last breath.

Your loving youngest daughter.

j) *Pages from old memories*

Many will see it as an article, but I see it as a book.

Here, I am presenting some memorable incidents of my Baba who was a great Palmist, Astrologer and a retired government servant from UPSC, my father Late Shri Iresh Chandra Dasgupta (B.A., B.T. from MC college, Syhlet, Bangladesh).

He was the second son of his parents. He grew up with uncles, aunts, cousins, and siblings. That was the time, joint family was very common. **Sona da** was referred to by all his younger brothers because he had an exceptionally kind heart.

Baba had lost his father at an early age of 12. His uncle took charge of his education. Baba was very intelligent and good at studies so his uncle helped him proceed with his education up to graduation and then BT (The degree is formerly known as Bachelor of Teaching and now B.Ed. Bachelor of Education).

Thereafter he joined the Bangladesh Army as an administrative officer. After independence and around the early 50s, he came to Delhi leaving the army and started his career in UPSC. But he was so intelligent and fast in his work that he finished his daily desk work within a few hours and made himself free for the rest of the day. So, he was free and available either in the canteen or under a big *peepal* tree near UPSC main gate (The tree is still present there) with a group of people, his subordinates and colleagues. He was popularly known as

"Dada" in his office. Soon it became a common practice that anyone looking for him during office hours would either find him in the canteen or under the *Peepal* tree. Before leaving office, he again ensured that he finished all remaining work (if any) so as not to keep any pending work for the next day.

He was not a devotee but he always visited different temples, gurdwaras, mosques, etc. He always said that if you purchase anything from within the temple premises, everything becomes prasad whether it is an offering to God or not. The vibes from temple premises itself is so pure and divine that everything becomes prasad.

In early 60s one fine day, he was sitting on the stairs of Bangla Sahib, Gurdwara, a Sikh gentleman walked past him in great haste and stress and at that particular moment my father said to him in hindi, " सरदारजी अंदर तो जा रहे हो, पर शांति नहीं मिलेगी" (sardarji, you are going inside but you will not find peace there). Sardarji went inside and prayed for quite some time but he truly did not get peace inside. Sardarji came out in search of the person who seemed to have understood his state of mind.

That was the first meeting of Baba and that Sikh man who was a renowned entrepreneur in hotel industries at that time. And thereafter he discussed all his problems with Baba and Baba gave him some remedies for his stress and anxiety. These remedies helped him a lot and he became a good friend of Baba. From that day onwards he started taking advice from Baba before starting any new project or any other issue.

Another friend of Baba was the owner of Paras cinema hall. He also took advice from Baba before starting the project. It was around 1970, that the project Paras cinema hall was started and at that time the Nehru Place was a complete jungle and the only attraction of that area was the Kalkaji temple. Baba said to him at that time in hindi, " ऐसा भी दिन आएगा जब चारो तरफ लोग ही लोग होंगे, बंजर नहीं रहेगा" (that this place is going to be most happening area of Delhi in the near future)

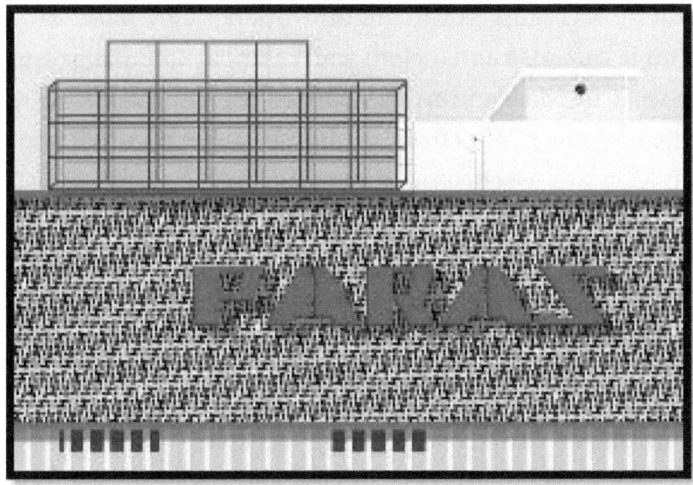

and advised him that he should carry on with his project here. After the completion of Paras cinema hall, my father used to get balcony passes. And we all were happy and excited when he got us free passes for the movies at the "Cinema Hall ".

Movies were referred to as Cinemas in those days and theatres were called "Cinema Halls"

We have seen many movies in Paras cinema hall "Rampur ka Lakhman", "Kora Kaagaj" and many more. And we have many fond memories of going to the cinema hall. It was like a picnic for us. Maa used to carry jam, bread, biscuits, light food, water and juices. Going to movies meant a complete fun package for kids like us. As soon as the movie got begin, we kids felt hungry and Maa used to put jam on bread and give us other foods items that she carried. Unlike these days we were allowed to carry homemade food to the Cinema Hall in those days. At that time, food available in the cinema hall were popcorn, burgers, Fanta and Cokes.

In the mid 70's, once a renowned industrialist came to Baba for his and his entire family horoscope. He came to our R. K. Puram quarter almost every day for more than 10 days. Maa was very innocent and thought that he was a big client so she prepared new dishes every day to please that industrialist client. The best part of the entire episode was when he was satisfied with all his work done by Baba, He gave a picture table calendar and a cloth wall calendar to Baba as a gesture. Baba gave it to Maa and as she opened all the calendars, she was shocked and threw it away from our house so that none of us could see it. When Maa was asked about the reason for her anger, she said that the calendar was all about naked ladies. At that time, we were kids and we didn't know the value of that calendar. The price of that calendar was huge in the international market but for us it went to the dustbin.

It was in the late 70's, after board exams were over a boy from our colony came to Baba with anxiety and asked whether he would pass the exam. Baba told him very casually that he would but when the result came out then he rushed to Baba and said very angrily that he got compartment in one subject. He shouted at Baba saying that his predictions were not correct and he used many other harsh words. Then Baba told him to calm down and said, "*had I told you after the exam about your result you would not have enjoyed your holidays thinking about the outcome …. Now you have enjoyed your holidays so work hard for your exam, you will definitely clear the paper.*"

Baba loved his children very much

It was an incident in the late 50's, the highly demanded gadget was the radio. At that time my elder sister was the only child of my parents. She just started talking and one fine morning, in her sweet broken words she said to Baba in Bengali, "***Baba, ladio chai***" (Baba, I want radio). Baba was so touched with her words that in the evening on the same day, Baba bought a Philip's radio for her. At that time, radio had a netted long antenna.

Another incident of the late 60's and early 70's, when we 5 children had summer vacation. My brothers were very naughty and always after Baba to take them to his office. They were not letting Baba leave for office. So, Baba took them to market, bought some jalebi and sometimes other things so that Baba could go to office. My eldest brother's favourite sweet was jalebi. He is now in his early 60s but still enjoys jelebi above all other sweets.

Baba and Modon Sadhu

Baba learned Palmistry and Astrology from Modon sadhu (a monk from Bangladesh) and was a great follower of Modon sadhu. Baba learned it at his young age out of passion only.

Due to his devotion to the monks, he was not interested in binding himself to a marriage contract. It was important for our grandma to tie that knot to her son so he could leave the monk's cell. She prayed to God and promised that when her second son married, she would worship an idol of "Bhairav" (an avatar of Shiva) the size of Baba's height. But he agreed to get married at a later age, our grandma was very happy to hear that news.

And as promised to God, our grandma ordered an idol of "Bhairav" the size of Baba's height and celebrated the puja of "Bhairav" at her house immediately after her son's marriage.

Baba was very naughty.

Whenever he was at home, we found him lying on his bed with all his belongings around him.

The following items were always kept near his bedside:

- Newspaper
- Spectacles
- Medicine box
- Latest panjika - Panjika is the Hindu astronomical almanac
- A trunk under his bed – full of books on palmistry, old panjika, etc.
- Tea cup

One fine evening, in early 80's Maa's close friend Ganguli mashima's son Monuda came to our Moti Bagh F block house to take Maa for a night stay at their Janakpuri house. When they were about to leave. Baba was so excited and opened his trunk and gave Rs 100/- to my brother to bring meat (only mutton, at that time we never had chicken in our kitchen). It means a party. At that time Baba said "***never show your weakness nor show that you have less money to an outsider***"

A touching moment of Love.

Baba's only anger was with Maa, and we children always complained about Maa to Baba. The most common complaint of us in Bengali was, "বাবা, মা দিচ্ছে না". (Baba, Maa is not giving). We never complained about Baba to Ma. We were so stupid at that time.

But when Baba was on death bed, he held Maa's hand and with compassionate eyes said sorry to her for all his anger. That was the most touching moment of Maa and Baba both.

Now, we lost both the parents and neither we have any complaint against Maa nor we have Baba to listen to our complaint.

Baba's Favourite:

Newspaper *The Statesman*

Cigarette *Cavanders*

Shoes *Bata*

Cloths *DCM*

Towel *Binny*

Woollen *Raymond*

Shopping *Connaught Place*

Cake, pastry, patties *Wengers*

Ice-cream, milk shake *Keventers*

Song *যৌবনসরসীনীরে মিলনশতদল. কোন্ চঞ্চল বন্যায় টলোমল টলোমল॥* (Jaubano sarosi nire Milano shatodal Kon chanchal bonyay talomolo talomol.)

As children, we enjoyed hearing the words "tolomolo, tolomolo"

Many more......

Baba believed that one shouldn't go with his horoscope.

You will be surprised to know that Baba didn't prepare horoscopes for any of his children.

Presented below are my interpretations from all of these realities, which have now become stories about Baba.

1. One should find his/her path.

2. Let it flow, let it go.

3. Embrace your life's excitement and enjoy every single moment.

4. Never fail to apologize for your wrongdoing or if you have hurt someone.

Part 2

Rhyme

1. Little Heart

A little heart can change your life.
A little heart can bring a smile to your face.
A little heart is within your body, keep it alive.
A single beat gives you a sense of life.
Keep on beating it, others may find their lives.
Oh! My little heart,
I LOVE YOU SO MUCH.
Little heart, o my little heart,
You are sweeter than the day before.
I cannot stop loving your sweetness.
You continue to make me
fall in love with you every day.

2. I have no regrets in my life

When I was a child, I was pampered by Baba.
When I was young,
I had good friends, siblings and cousins.
who always made me happy.
Though we had fought for silly things,
Now I'm laughing over it.
I have no regrets in my life.

Now that I am in middle age,
Have been pampered by my daughter.
And, going to be a senior citizen very soon.
I'm hoping to celebrate it.
and will cherish my good golden Era of life.
I have no regrets in my life.

I will leave this world with a happy note.
I lived my life in heaven
And, wanted to tell this world
Heaven is here only.
Just open your eyes,
you will find heaven around you.
I have no regrets in my life.

3. I am rich, I won't cry

I am rich, but I am not a multi-millionaire - I won't cry.
I am rich, but I don't have a fancy car - I won't cry.
I am rich, but I don't have a luxurious house - I won't cry.
I am rich, but I don't travel the world - I won't cry.
I am rich, but I don't earn a lot of money - I won't cry.
I am rich, but I don't have too many friends - I won't cry.
I am rich, but I didn't excel in my job - I won't cry.
I am rich, but I have very little knowledge - I won't cry.
I am rich, but I can't impress people - I won't cry.
I am rich, but I am not beautiful - I won't cry.

Yes, I am rich.
I have got tremendous love from Maa and Baba
since my birth.
I am now receiving extraordinary love
from my daughter.
I am the richest,
Love makes me the richest,
I won't cry.

4. Life

Life is beautiful,
when you get things without any effort.
Life is challenging,
when you earn your desires.
Life is exciting,
when you live on your own terms.
Life is dull,
without challenges and excitements.
Life is powerful,
when you create it.
Life is easy,
when you know the route.
Life is adventurous,
when you explore a new route.
Life is a puzzle,
when you solve it.
Life is full of thrills,
when you find a way to overcome them.
Life is stressful,
when you are trying to reach your destination on time;
but unable to reach because of obstacles on your route.

Adapt your life to the way you perceive it.

5. Time is flying

Time is flying - We can't hold time.
We can only hold it in - our memories.

Good time or bad time,
Let it be decided by our memories.
Time is flying - We can't hold time.
We can only hold it in - our memories.

Do good work, Keep good relations,
Memory will hold your time.
Time is flying - We can't hold time.
We can only hold it in - our memories.

As long as we have memories,
We can travel anywhere at any time.
Time is flying - We can't hold time.
We can only hold it in - our memories.

Yes, we can hold time in our memories.

6. "Maa"

First touch.
First friend.
First teacher.
First tailor.
First cook.
First designer.
First make-up artist.
First guide.
First love.
First inspiration.
First adviser.
First word "Maa".

        Maa is a complete sentence.
        Maa is a complete paragraph.
        Maa is a complete chapter.
        Maa is a complete book.

Each day is a new story.
Each life has many episodes -
Child, teen, adult, middle age and old.
But the role of Maa always remains the same.

        Maa – the most affectionate lady of our house.
        We all should learn from her –
        how to give love and be a good human.

"Maa"

Maa and Diya,
one ushered me on this earth and one gave me the same bliss.
Both are very special in my life.

While I do not consider myself to be beautiful,
my daughter always makes me feel as if
I am the queen of the world's beauty pageant.

While I do not consider myself to be cute,
my daughter always makes me feel like
I am the cutest person in the world.

It is only a pure heart
that can discern my innermost feelings.

"Maa"

Maa, I want to share a secret
with you today,
when I was in your womb
I could hear only your heartbeats.
Now,
I have the same heartbeats,
you have transferred to me during my birth.

And,
you are living in each beat of my heart.

7. Last words from a person on death bed

I have nothing left to give to anyone anymore.

I have found a way where I will be happy and safe.

At this moment of time,
I can hear the last whistle from God
to end this life race.

I am ending my life journey,
Just recollect all precious moments
spend with you.

Goodbye to my beautiful world,
I am the winner and arrived
at the end point of the race.

Please don't bring tears on your eyes,
don't let them roll down on your cheeks,
as I live in every drop of them.

Love you all.

8. Choose a caption

\# Everything changes, but laughter remains the same.

\# Laughter can neither be created nor destroyed.

\# Laughter is a fountain of happiness.

\# Laughter makes others happy.

\# Laughter is a therapy which releases all pain.

\# Why keep laughing Buddha at home,
when you can laugh like Buddha at home.

কবিতা ও গান

১. আমার বিশ্বাস

আমি আছি, তুমি আছো
এতো আমার অগাধ বিশ্বাস।

আমিতে তুমি আছো,
এইটা আমার দৃঢ় বিশ্বাস।
তোমাতে আমি আছি
সেটা নয় আমার বিশ্বাস।

তুমি হারালে, আমি তোমায় খুঁজে পাবো,
এইটা আমার বিশ্বাস।
আমি হারালে, তুমি আমায় খুঁজে পাবে,
সেটা নয় আমার বিশ্বাস।

আমার প্রারম্ভিক বিন্দুতে বিদ্যমান তুমি,
এইটা আমার বিশ্বাস।
তোমার প্রারম্ভিক বিন্দুতে বিদ্যমান আমি,
সেটা নয় আমার বিশ্বাস।

আমি-তুমি তে কোথাও,
একটা লুকো-চুরি খেলা আছে
এইটা আমার বিশ্বাস।
তুমি-আমি তে মিল আছে,
সেটা নয় আমার বিশ্বাস।
তুমি-আমি তে মিল আছে,
সেটা নয় আমার বিশ্বাস।

২. ভালোবাসার গান

কতো দূরে থাকো, তবু হৃদয়ে আছো।
কোনো দেখা যে নেই, তবু জানি তুমি আছো।

"এ কি ভালোবাসা, প্রিয়া "
"তুমি বলো প্রিয়, বলো না গো"।

জানি এক দিন দেখা হবে,
দেখো চিনতে ভুলো না মোরে।

কতো দূরে থাকো, তবু হৃদয়ে আছো।
কোনো দেখা যে নেই, তবু জানি তুমি আছো।

"এ কি ভালোবাসা, প্রিয়া "
"তুমি বলো প্রিয়, বলো না গো"।

যদি যেতে চাই দূরে, জানি তুমি বাধা দেবে মোরে।

কতো দূরে থাকো, তবু হৃদয়ে আছো।
কোনো দেখা যে নেই, তবু জানি তুমি আছো।

"এ কি ভালোবাসা, প্রিয়া "
"তুমি বলো প্রিয়, বলো না গো"।

৩. মা ও সন্তান

সন্তানের সাথে,
মার সম্পর্ক ন-মাস বেশি।
তাইতো,
মার কাছে থাকে সন্তান চিরঋণী।

সন্তানকে বড়ো হতে অনুভব করেন,
শুধু মা তার গর্ভে।
তাইতো,
মা বুঝতে পারেন সন্তানের ব্যথা অতি সহজে।

সন্তান কে মা সবসময় আশীর্বাদ করেন,
"দীর্ঘজীবী হও"
কিন্তু সন্তান কোনো দিনও বলে না,
"মা, তুমি দীর্ঘজীবী হও।"
তাইতো,
মা আমাদের ছেড়ে চলে গেলেন ,
অতি সহজে।

মা, তুমি কি জানো
তোমার হৃদয়ের স্পন্দন
আমি শুনতে পেরেছিলাম তোমার গর্ভে।
তাইতো,
আমার হৃদয় স্পন্দনে আজ ও তুমি আছো
চিরস্থায়ী হয়ে।

৪. অণু

অণু,
তুমি খুব ক্ষুদ্র, তুমি খুব ছোটো,
তোমায় চোখে দেখা যায় না।
কিন্তু, তুমি আছো সকলের মাঝে।

অণু, তুমি আছো
জলে, স্থলে, আকাশে, বাতাসে, পাহাড়ে, নদীতে,
গাছের পাতায়, গাছের ফুলে, মানুষের মাঝে।

অণু,
তুমি খুব ক্ষুদ্র, তুমি খুব ছোটো,
তোমায় চোখে দেখা যায় না।
কিন্তু, তুমি আছো সকলের মাঝে।

অণু, তুমি আছো
এই পৃথিবী জুড়ে,
তুমিই সবাই কে জুড়ে রেখেছো,
তুমি ছাড়া কিছুই নেই,
কিছুই থাকবে না,
কিছুই হবে না,
কিছুই জুড়বে না।

অণু,
তুমি খুব ক্ষুদ্র, তুমি খুব ছোটো,
তোমায় চোখে দেখা যায় না।
কিন্তু, তুমি আছো সকলের মাঝে।

शायरी

१. ज़िंदगी की तलाश

जंहा पर खत्म हुई मोहब्बतें इश्क की,
वहीं से शुरू हुई दास्ताने गम की।
अब हाल कुछ ऐसा हुआ ~

जीने की तलाश में, जीना ही भूल गई।
हँसने की तलाश में, हँसना ही भूल गई।

ज़िंदगी की तलाश में, ज़िंदा रहना ही भूल गई।

ऊंचाई की तलाश में, नीचे देखना भूल गई।
आगे बढ़ने की तलाश में, पीछे मुड़ना भुल गई।

ज़िंदगी की तलाश में, ज़िंदा रहना ही भूल गई।

ख़ुशी की तलाश में, कब ख़ुशी आई,
और पता भी ना चला रूठ के चली गई।
पर,
रोने के तलाश करें बिना,
आँखों में आँसु आये
और गालों से गुजर के बहने लगे।

ज़िंदगी की तलाश में, ज़िंदा रहना ही भूल गई।

२. माँ, तू तो माँ है

माँ, तू तो माँ है।
तू है, तो हमारी दुनिया पूरी है।
जन्म दिया, पाला पोसा बड़ा किया हमें।
माँ, तूने कहा भगवान है,
हमने भी माना भगवान है।
पर, भगवान से बड़ी हमारी माँ है।

माँ तू है, तो हमारी दुनिया पूरी है।

प्यार करना सीखा तुझसे।
गले लगाना सीखा तुझसे।
संसार को जोड़ के रखना सीखा तुझसे।
तुझसे जो सीखा,
वह किसी किताब में नहीं पाया
और नहीं किसी ओर ने हमें सिखाया।

माँ तू है, तो हमारी दुनिया पूरी है।

माँ, तू क्यों इतनी जल्दी चली गई।
कुछ पल और साथ देती,
बहुत कुछ तुझसे सीखना हे बाकी।
भटकती राहो में खड़े हे हम अभी भी,
सही दिशा दिखाना था, तुझे ही।

माँ तू है, तो हमारी दुनिया पूरी है।

तेरे स्पर्श से सारा गम भूल जाते थे हम।
तेरे हॅसते हुए चेहरे देख के,
तुझे, आनंद से लिपट जाते थे हम।
अब तु ही बता तेरा स्पर्श पाने के लिए,
किस के पास जाए हम।
तेरा स्पर्श हर दुःख का निवारण है, माँ।

माँ तू है, तो हमारी दुनिया पूरी है।

माँ, तुझे एक बात कहनी थी,
तेरे हृदय स्पंदन सुना था,
तेरे कोंख में जब मैं थी।
पर,
तुझे ये बात कभी कह ना पाई।
अब तू जहां है,
ये बात तुझ तक पहुंचना
मुश्किल है।
तेरी हृदय स्पंदन के साथ तूने मुझे जन्म दिया
मैं हूं तो मेरे साथ तू भी है
और
माँ, तू है, तो हमारी दुनिया पूरी है।

माँ, तूने कहा भगवान है,
हमने भी माना भगवान है।
पर, भगवान से बड़ी हमारी माँ है।

३. हमने देखी है दुनिया, बदल ते हुए

हमने देखी है दुनिया, बदल ते हुए।

एक पैसा, दो पैसा कॉइन से
दस रुपया, बीस रुपया का कॉइन हाँथो में लेते हुए।

हमने देखी है दुनिया, बदल ते हुए।
पॉकेट में रुपये के बदले क्रेडिट कार्ड और डेबिट कार्ड रखते हुए।

हमने देखी है दुनिया, बदल ते हुए।
डाकिया डाक लाता था ७ से १० दिन में,
अब ईमेल कुछ ही सेकंड में डिलीवरी होते हुए।

हमने देखी है दुनिया, बदल ते हुए।
दुसरे शहर में बात करने के लिए,
कॉल बुक करते थे कई घंटे पहले;
अब डायल करो तो तुरंत मिल जाते है
इंटरनेट कॉल के ज़रिये।

हमने देखी है दुनिया, बदल ते हुए।
पोस्ट ऑफिस पर ट्रंक कॉल, टेलीग्राम ख़त्म होते हुए।

हमने देखी है दुनिया, बदल ते हुए।
ग्रामोफोन से टेप रिकॉर्डर लाते हुए।
टेप रिकॉर्डर से सीडी, ब्लूटूथ, पेन ड्राइव,
म्यूजिक सिस्टम उपयोग करते हुए।

हमने देखी है दुनिया, बदल ते हुए।
रेडियो एंटीना से टीवी एंटीना हिलाते हुए।
टीवी एंटीना से डिश टीवी लगाते हुए।

हमने देखी है दुनिया, बदल ते हुए।
ब्लैक एन व्हाइट टीवी से कलर्ड टीवी लाते हुए।
कलर्ड टीवी से स्मार्ट टीवी परिवर्तन होते हुए।

हमने देखी है दुनिया, बदल ते हुए।
टाइपराइटर से कंप्यूटर चलाते हुए।
कंप्यूटर से लैपटॉप पर काम करते हुए।

हमने देखी है दुनिया, बदल ते हुए।
फ्लॉपी ड्राइव से सीडी ड्राइव होते हुए।
सीडी ड्राइव से पेन ड्राइव, मेमोरी कार्ड स्लॉट आते हुए।

हमने देखी है दुनिया, बदल ते हुए।
MS-DOS ऑपरेटिंग सिस्टम से Windows पर काम करते हुए।
ब्लैक एन व्हाइट मॉनिटर से एलईडी मॉनिटर होते हुए।

हमने देखी है दुनिया, बदल ते हुए।
१० साल बाद सब पार्ट अप्रचलित होते हुए।
हर दूसरे दिन कुछ नया अपडटेस आते हुए।

हमने देखी है दुनिया, बदल ते हुए।
की-बोर्ड से टच स्क्रीन उपयोग करते हुए।
लैपटॉप से आई-पैड उपयोग करते हुए।

हमने देखी है दुनिया, बदलते हुए।
इंडोर गेम से वीडियो गेम खेलते हुए।
इंडोर गेम खेलते थे पास-पास बैठे हुए।
कभी-कभी पकड़े जाते थे चीटिंग करते हुए।
ऑनलाइन गेम आया,
इंडोर गेम का परिभाषा बदल गया ।

हमने देखी है दुनिया, बदल ते हुए।
जॉइंट फैमिली से न्यूक्लियर फैमिली होते हुए।
बचपन बिता साथ-साथ, अब वह भाई बहन
सिब्लिंग्स और कजिन्स कहते हुए।

हमने देखी है दुनिया, बदल ते हुए।
अंगीठी से गैस स्टोव पर खाना बनते हुए।
अब माइक्रो ओवन, इंडक्शन कुकटॉप लाते हुए।

हमने देखी है दुनिया, बदल ते हुए।
५ पैसा से ५ रुपये बस टिकट होते हुए।
सैलरी पैकेज ४ फिगर से
५ फिगर, ६ फिगर, ७ फिगर, ८ फिगर होते हुए।

हमने देखी है दुनिया, बदल ते हुए।
न्यूज़ सुबह-शाम से पूरे दिन आते हुए।
टीवी सीरियल साप्ताहिक से रोजाना होते हुए।
रोजाना से नेटफ्लिक्स, अमाजॉन प्राइम
कभी भी अपने टाइम पर देखते हुए।

हमने देखी है दुनिया, बदल ते हुए।
पैदल, साइकिल और बस पर चलने वाले
आज गाड़ी के बिना चल नहीं पाते,

गाड़ी से उतार कर जिम जाते,
ट्रेड मिल में पैदल चलने के लिए।
साइकिल चलाने के लिए,
क्योंकि फिट रहना भी ज़रूरी है जीने के लिए।

हमने देखी है दुनिया, बदल ते हुए।
बस एक पड़ोसी के घर का टेलीफोन
पूरे मोहल्ला का संपर्क नंबर होते हुए।
हमने देखा है पड़ोसी को तंग होते हुए।
अब घरो में लैंडलाइन, मोबाइल और इंटरनेट से
पड़ोसियो की परेशानियाँ दूर जाती हुई।
अब, हाल कुछ ऐसा हुआ -
मोबाइल नहीं, इंटरनेट नहीं हो,
तो, थम जाती है हमारी दुनिया।

हमने देखी है दुनिया, बदल ते हुए।
लैंडलाइन फ़ोन से पेजर आते हुए।
पेजर से मोबाइल फ़ोन आते हुए।
मोबाइल पर इनकमिंग कॉल चार्ज देते हुए।
२जी ३जी ४जी ५जी में तबदीली होते हुए।

हमने देखी है दुनिया, बदल ते हुए।
शॉपिंग भी ऑनलाइन होते हुए।
विंडो शॉपिंग से वेबसाइट सर्चिंग होते हुए।

हमने देखी है दुनिया, बदल ते हुए।
पुस्तक ढूँढ़नी है तो लाइब्रेरी जाते थे।
अब वह पुस्तक किंडल पर मिल जाते है,
या गूगल पर सर्च करो,
ऑनलाइन भी खरीद सकते है।

कुछ तो फ्री डाउनलोड भी करते है।

हमने देखी है दुनिया, बदल ते हुए।
समाचार सुन ना है, तो कहो, एलेक्सा–समाचार।
मौसम का हाल पूछना है, तो कहो, एलेक्सा-मौसम।
आज का तापमान जानना है, तो कहो, एलेक्सा-तापमान।
रिलैक्स करना है, तो कहो, एलेक्सा-लाइट म्यूजिक।
पार्टी करना है, तो कहो, एलेक्सा-पार्टी गाना।
अलार्म सेट करना है, तो कहो, एलेक्सा-अलार्म।
अगर भूल जाने की आदत है,
तो रिमाइंडर सेट करो, एलेक्सा-रिमाइंड।

हमने देखी है दुनिया, बदल ते हुए।
अब तो हमारे पास हर एक चीज़ स्मार्ट है
स्मार्ट लाइट,
स्मार्ट फैन,
स्मार्ट मोबाइल,
स्मार्ट टीवी,
स्मार्ट वाच।

हमने देखी है दुनिया, बदल ते हुए।
पहले की कठिनाइयाँ जाते हुए।
और नयी कठिनाइयाँ उभरते हुए।

हमने देखी है दुनिया, बदल ते हुए।
नई पीढ़ी के लिए एक नया कहानी रचते हुए।

४. अधूरा सपना

आज एक अधूरा सपना देखा।
रंग बिरंगे तितलियों को उड़ते हुए देखा।

मैं भी उनके साथ उड़ रही थी।
उड़ते उड़ते उनके घर पँहुची।

देखा फूलों से भरा आंगन उनका।
छू ने लगी,
तो पीछे से आवाज़ आयी किसी की।
"छुना नहीं, रंग उतर जाएगा।
तोड़ना नहीं, पौधा रूठ जाएगा।"

मैं तितलियों के रंगसे रंगने लगी थी,
पर, अचानक नींद खुली
और बिस्तर से नीचे गिरी।

ढल गया रंग अंग का,
ढूंढ़ने लगी घर तितलियों का।

वह अधूरा सपना,
छोड़ गया रंग, तितलियों का।
वह अधूरा सपना,
छोड़ गया रंग, तितलियों का।

५. झूठा ख़्वाब

अजीब दस्ताये मोहब्बत की है।

इश्क़ है, पर इज़हार ना कर पाए।
जब दूर हुए, जान पाए;
वह इश्क़, इश्क़ नहीं था,
एक झूठा ख़्वाब था ।

ख़्वाब देखो,
पर आँखे बंद ना करो।
दिल, दिमाग़ और आँखे खोल कर जियो।

दिल ने कहा,
दिमाग ने सोचा,
आँखों ने देखा,
वह ख़्वाब नहीं, वह जीवन की सच्चाई है।

ख़्वाब देखो वही,
जो हक़ीक़त हो जाए कभी।

६. ज़िन्दगी है

ज़िन्दगी है - एक लेख,
कुछ हो जाए गलती और कुछ बन गई पंक्ति।

ज़िन्दगी है - एक कविता,
कुछ शायर हो गए और कुछ गायक बन गए।

ज़िन्दगी है - एक रंग मंच,
कुछ परदे के पीछे रह गए और कुछ नायक बन गए।

ज़िन्दगी है - एक गीत
कुछ बादशाह सुरों के हो गए और कुछ सम्राट ताल के बन गए।

ज़िन्दगी है, तो इंसान है।
ऊपरवाले ने क्या ख़ूब इंसान बनाया,
कुछ खलनायक बन जाते है और कुछ फ़रिस्ते रह जाते है।
कुछ खलनायक बन जाते है और कुछ फ़रिस्ते रह जाते है।

७. आप, इंसान हो, मेरे दोस्त

हर चीज़ खरीदी नहीं जाता, मेरे दोस्त।
आप, व्यापारी नहीं हो ज़िन्दगी कें;
आप, इंसान हो, मेरे दोस्त।

खुद को ना बेचो,
बस एतबार, अपने पर रखो, मेरे दोस्त।
कोई व्यापारी नहीं है, इस दुनिया में,
जो ख़रीद पाए आपको।

कुछ चीज़ पाया,
और कुछ महसूस भी किया जाता है, मेरे दोस्त।
प्यार, मोहब्बत वह चीज़ है,
जहाँ मोल-भाव नहीं होता है।

कुछ पल अपने लिए भी जी लो, मेरे दोस्त।
दिल खुश करो किसी ओर का।
पर, मुस्कान अपने चेहरे से,
जाने ना दो, मेरे दोस्त।

ये दिन भी गुज़र जायेगा, मेरे दोस्त।
पर, ये पल याद रह जायेगा।
बस इतना ख्याल रखना, मेरे दोस्त।
आप, व्यापारी नहीं हो ज़िन्दगी कें;
आप, इंसान हो, मेरे दोस्त।

८. एक मुसाफ़िर

हम, एक मुसाफ़िर है, ज़िन्दगी, सुहाना सफ़र है।
थक कर, बैठना, ना कभी।
रुक कर, हार मानना, ना कभी।
लम्बी-सी डगर है,
चलना है बहुत दूर अभी।
मंजिल का फॉर्म - भरना बाक़ी है अभी।

हम, एक मुसाफ़िर है, ज़िन्दगी, सुहाना सफ़र है।
बचपन बीता – चलते-चलते,
जवानी बीती – भागते-भागते,
बुढ़ापा, बीत रहा है – धीमे-धीमे,
चलना है बहुत दूर अभी।
मंजिल का फॉर्म - भरना बाक़ी है अभी।

हम, एक मुसाफ़िर है, ज़िन्दगी, सुहाना सफ़र है।
दुनिया में आए - रोते-रोते।
सफ़र ज़िन्दगी का पूरा हुआ -
खुशियाँ बटोरते-बटोरते।

कोई गम ना होगा साथ,
दुनिया छोड़ देंगे -
अब, हँसते-हँसते, गाते-गाते।

हम, एक मुसाफ़िर है, ज़िन्दगी, सुहाना सफ़र है।

९. सन्नाटा और खामोशी

देखो, आज कुछ नया, करने का मन हो रहा है।
आओ चलो,
सन्नाटा और खामोशी की बातें, चुपके से सुनते हैं।

खामोशी, सन्नाटे से प्यार भरी नज़रों से, कह रही है,
"तुम क्यों उदास हो जानेमन,
तुम तो मेरी जान हो।
ओ सुनो टिक-टिक करती
घड़ी की आवाज़, कुछ कह रही है।
धूम मचाते रहो, गिने चुने पल हैं।
समय कब हो जाए पूरा,
किसी को कुछ नहीं पता।
समय से पहले - कभी सोना नहीं।
समय से पहले - कभी खोना नहीं। "

यह सुन के, सन्नाटे ने खामोशी से कहा,
"तुम ही हो प्यार मेरा,
तुम्हारे बिना हूँ मैं अधुरा।
धड़क-धड़क वह दिल की धड़कन,
कुछ कह रही है।
आज तुम इतने करीब आ जाओ,
दुरियाँ, ना रहें कोई।
गुम हो जाए, एक दूसरे में ऐसे,
की फ़ासला, ना रहे कोई।"

तभी, हवा का आवारा झोंका आया,
और दिल की बातों को उड़ा ले गया।

ना रहा सन्नाटा, ना रही खामोशी।
बातें उनकी ना हो पाईं पूरी।

मिलेंगे फुर्सत में फिर कभी,
जंहा हवा का आवारा झोंका,
मिल ना पाए उनसे कभी।

१०. एक नई सुबह

ये पल, कब गुज़र गया,
पता भी ना चला।
अगर, दिन ना गुज़र जाता,
और रात का अँधेरा छा ना जाता।

एक और भी है, हक़ीक़त ~
पल पल बीत जाने से,
दिन का भी होता है अंत।

एक नई सुबह, आएगी।
उम्मीद की ये सुबह,
फिरसे, रंग लाएगी।

अलफ़ाज़ से भरी होगी,
दास्ताने इश्क़ की।
ना होगा - गिला शिकवा कोई,
ना होगा - गम कोई।

अलफ़ाज़ से भरा होगा हर पल,
बस साथ रहना, मेरे हमसफ़र।

११. नया दिन

बैठे थे, अंधेरे में।
अचानक, रोशनी आँखों
में चुभने लगी।

बाहर आई,
तो देखा, सवेरा हो गया।
पंछी का चहकना,
पतंग जैसे उड़ना,
नीले आसमान पर, सूरज की
पहेली किरण उभर आना।

शुरू हो गया,
एक नया दिन,
ले आई खुशबू
ले आई उम्मीद,
ले आई
खुशियाँ नई-नई।

इश्क, मोहब्बत और प्रेम
से भरलो दामन किसी का।
कहीं बीत ना जाए
यह सुनहरा दिन आज का।

१२. नन्हे फ़रिस्ते

धरती के कोंख से जन्म लेते हुए,
वो पहली किरण सूरज की।

जैसे, माँ के कोंख से,
जन्म हुआ नन्हे फ़रिस्ते का।

सुबह की रोशनी से, रौशन हुआ,
जीवन फ़रिस्ते का।

सूरज की किरणों से, सीखा -
शांत, नटखट, लड़कपन, ज़िन्दगी का।

तपती, कड़कती, धूप ने दिया -
शोला जवानी का।

ढलते हुए सूरज ने कहा,
"वक्त हुआ जाने का",
"वक्त हुआ जाने का"।

१३. तस्वीर

गुज़रा हुआ पल,
एक तस्वीर था - समय का।

आने वाला पल,
एक तस्वीर होगा - समय का।

जो पल जी रहे हैं,
वो भी एक तस्वीर है - समय का।

चलो, इन तस्वीरों में रंग भरते हैं।

देखो कोई रंग, छूट ना जाए,
किसी का।
जीवन रंगो का मेला है,
भर दो दामन, रंगो से सब का।

वो गुज़रा हुआ पल,
जी लेंगे फिरसे।
जब बरसेंगी - रंग बिरंगी यादें,
इन तस्वीरों में।

समये के, इन तस्वीरों से –
कभी झुक ना पाएंगे हम।
जो सच्चाई छुपी है, इन तस्वीरों में –
उनसे कभी मुकर ना पाएंगे हम।

१४. यह सफ़र

हमारा सफ़र, आप के साथ,
इतना ही था।

जो सफ़र, आप के साथ रहा,
बहुत ही खूबसूरत था।

दोस्त हज़ार मिलेंगे राहो में ,
पर, दिल लगी, किसी एक से होगी।
वह छूट जाए,
तो, दिल में आग लग जाएगी।
बरस बीत जायेगा,
पर, आग ना निभ पाएगी।

इस सफ़र में, आपने हमें कुछ सिखाया,
कुछ, हमने आप को सिखाया।
बचपन फिर से जी लिया।
प्यार, मोहब्बत सामने देखा,
तो, हाथ बढ़ाना सिख लिया।

जिंदगी रही - तो फिर मिलेंगे,
यादो में - आप सदा रहेंगे ।
आगे चलके, साथ मिले
या ना मिले,
पर, पूरा किया साथ-साथ हमने यह सफ़र,
अब चाहे मानो हमें गैर या हमसफ़र ।

१५. पचपन और बचपन

मिले पचपन में;
वो बचपन की सखि।
जिंदगी कहने लगी,
"जी ले फिरसे पचपन में बचपन आपनी"

ये वह सखि है,
जिन्होंनें सिखाया हंसना, खिलखिलाना।
दूर - रहकर भी,
पास होने का एहसास दिलाया।

उमर तो हो रही है,
पर, बचपन की सखि ने,
बढ़ने नहीं दिया।
अब देखो,
पचपन और बचपन,
चलने लगे साथ-साथ।

१६. मिलते थे हमें भी ख़त

लिखते थे ख़त, हम भी; कभी-कभी।
मिलते थे हमें भी ख़त, किसी का; कभी-कभी।
किसी का ख़त आने का इंतज़ार,
करते थे हम भी; कभी-कभी।
जब नहीं मिलता था ख़त,
तो जान निकल जाती थी; कभी-कभी।

"कोई ख़त आया क्या हमारा",
डाकिया से पूछा करते थे; कभी-कभी।
जब वह देने लागते थे ख़त हाथो में,
ख़ुशी, आँखों में झलक आती थी; तभी तभी।
इंतज़ार का घड़ी ख़त्म होता था,
और पढ़ने लगते थे ख़त; तभी तभी।

लिखते थे ख़त, हम भी; कभी-कभी।
मिलते थे हमें भी ख़त, किसी का; कभी-कभी।

जो ख़ुशी, लिखने में आती थी,
वह चाहे एक सादा पन्ना हो,
या कोई एक पीला पोस्टकार्ड,
नहीं तो, नीला इनलैंड लेटर भी,
होता था; कभी-कभी।

लिखते थे ख़त, हम भी; कभी-कभी।
मिलते थे हमें भी ख़त, किसी का; कभी-कभी।

दुःखों का आसमान भी,
टूट जाता था; कभी-कभी ।
दिल की ख्वाइश भी,
होती थी पूरी; कभी-कभी ।

जाने वह दिन कँहा खो गए।
ना आती है, दिल से लिखी हुई ख़त कोई।
ना रहता है, इंतज़ार किसी ख़त का कोई।

आज के नए दौर में,
ख़त लिखने की आदत छूट ने लगी ।
मैसेज और ईमेल,
ख़त के नए रूप में उभर ने लगी ।

लिखते थे ख़त, हम भी; कभी-कभी।
मिलते थे हमें भी ख़त, किसी का; कभी-कभी।

१७. सफल करो सपना

मैंने देखा है सपना, बंद आँखों से।
पूरे होते ना देखा, कभी खुले आँखों से।

जो देखा मैंने सपना - खुली आँखों से,
नज़र आता है, वह, अब पूरा होते हुए।

आता है, सपना - बहुत ख़्यालओ में मेरे,
पर, ख़्याल कभी नसीब ना हुआ - सपनों में मेरे।

सपना पूरा होने का आस था - जिन्हे,
वो, अब, नींद से कोशो दूर रहते परे।

देखो, आज का समय क्या कह रहा है,
उठो, जागो, सफल करो – सपना, अपने लिए।

उठो, जागो सफल करो – सपना, अपने लिए।

१८. तन्हा एक सोच है

तन्हा-तन्हा - आँखे बंद, खामोशियो में बैठी थी।

"तुम तन्हा नहीं हो", दूर से एक आवाज़ आई - धीमी सी।

पास जा कर देखा, एक अक्षर - मुस्कुराता हुआ नज़र आया।

मैंने बोला, "तुम क्या जानो, तन्हा है क्या?
अक्षर-अक्षर के साथ मिलते हो, तो शब्द पूरा हो जाता है।
शब्द-शब्द से मिलके, पंक्ति बन जाती है।
पंक्ति पुरा होता है, तो, एक नयी कविता बन जाती है।"

अक्षर ने कहा, "अक्षर-अक्षर को मिला कर, शब्द पूरा किया तुमने।
शब्दों से पंक्ति बनायी तुमने, पंक्ति पूरी की,
और एक नयी कविता, लिख डाली - तुमने।
क्या तुम, अभी भी तन्हा हो"?
"तुम नहीं जानते, कोई तन्हा नहीं है।
दोस्तों से मिलते हो,
तो, खुशियों की बहार आ जाती है।
हंसी के फुब्बारे निकलते है।
तुम दोस्तों से मिल कर,
एक पलटन में समा जाते हो।
तन्हा एक सोच है,
गुजरा हुआ पल है।
सोच बदलो, दोस्तों से मिलो।"

१९. ऐसे दर्द भी है

एक नई पहचान के साथ, आयी हूँ।
आप को कुछ सुनाना चाहती हूँ।

दर्द - चाहे कुछ भी हो,
मुस्कुराकर दर्द को भूलना चाहती हूँ।

मेरे अंदर जो दर्द छुपा है,
उस दर्द से, राहत पाना चाहती हूँ।

भले, मैं आप के कुछ काम ना आ पाऊँ,
पर, आप के प्रति नाज़ होना चाहती हूँ।

ऐसे दर्द भी है,
जो समय के साथ - मिट जाते है।
पर, कुछ दर्द ऐसे भी है,
जो समय के साथ - बढ़ जाते है।

दर्द में दुबी शाम,
अक्सर बह जाते है - जाम में।
और जो रह जाए दर्द,
वह, बह जाते है - आंसू में।

बह दर्द, दर्द नहीं कहलाये,
जो, आंसू के मोती बन कर, बह ना जाए।

२०. मेरी परछाई

ज़मीन में - मेरी परछाई,
हँसते हुए, कह रही है,
"आज, मुझे देख लो,
कल तुम्हारी बारी है।
मिट्टी में मिलने की,
किसी की ख़्वाहिश नहीं होती है।
पर, हकीकत यही है,
कि मिट्टी में मिलना सबको एक दिन है।
जब तुम मिट्टी में मिलोगे,
तो, ये परछाई लौट कर नहीं आएगी। "

यही है सच्चाई,
मैं और मेरी परछाई।

परछाई भी बहुत अनोखी है,
अंधेरे में साथ छोड़ देती है।

कहने को तो अपनी है।
पर, अंतिम यात्रा में वह भी,
साथ छोड़ देती है।

यही है सच्चाई,
मैं और मेरी परछाई।

२१. सिंपल लाइफ

कोई लौटा दे मेरे - वो बचपन के दिन।
जहां प्यार ही प्यार था, बहुत ही सिंपल लाइफ थी।

अपना तो, एंटरटेनमेंट, बस टी बी पर,
बुधवार का चित्रहार और रविवार का मूवी थी।
साल में, दो बार हॉल में,
परिवार के साथ मूवी देखना अनिवार्य था।
हॉल जाने के दिन - अपना बेस्ट ड्रेस पहनते थे,
और स्नैक्स पैक करके ले जाते थे।
मूवी देखते-देखते - स्नैक्स खाते थे,
मूवी देखते-देखते - डायलॉग्स याद करते थे,
और, वापस आते टाइम
उसी मूवी के डायलाग दोहराते थे।

कोई लौटा दे मेरे - वो बचपन के दिन।
जहां प्यार ही प्यार था, बहुत ही सिंपल लाइफ थी।

तब स्कूल भी - क्या स्कूल था।
पढ़ाई, मस्ती और पनिशमेंट साथ-साथ चलते थे।
लेट होने पर गेट बंद हो जाता था।
फिर, रिक्बेस्ट कर के, स्कूल के अंदर जाना होता था।
नहीं तो, कोई सीक्रेट एंट्री से - स्कूल के अंदर जाते थे,
और फिर दोस्तों को अपना चौड़ दिखाते थे।

कभी-कभी, क्लास में लेट हो जाते थे,
कभी-कभी, होमवर्क पूरा कर नहीं पाते थे,
तो, टीचर का डाट खाना पड़ता था ।
पनिशमेंट मिले, कभी मुर्गा बनना पड़ता था,
या बेंच पर खड़े होना पड़ता था।
बेंच पर खड़े होने का, मज़ा ही कुछ और आता था,
सबसे ऊपर हम थे,
बाकि सब नीचे पढ़ने में, बेहाल होते थे ।
और कभी, क्लास रूम से बाहर,
होने का भी पनिशमेंट मिलता था,
तो मानो लाटरी लग जाती थी -
उसी टाइम दौड़ के, खेलने चले जाते थे प्लेग्राउंड पे।

कोई लौटा दे मेरे - वो बचपन के दिन।
जहां प्यार ही प्यार था, बहुत ही सिंपल लाइफ थी।

ठीक से पढ़ाई ना करने पर, माँ की डॉट पड़ति थी,
और कभी-कभी,
"ना खेलने जाना और ना ही दोस्तों से मिलना",
धमकी भी मिलती थी।

शाम को खेलने जाते थे - तो कंडीशन भी साथ था,
"स्ट्रीट लाइट जलने से पहले घर के अंदर आना" ।
तब नहीं कोई मेकअप, बस कोई भी ड्रेस पहन के
जल्दी से घर के बाहर दोस्तों से मिलने जाते थे।

कोई लौटा दे मेरे - वो बचपन के दिन।
जहां प्यार ही प्यार था, बहुत ही सिंपल लाइफ थी।

किसी के घर,
किसी भी वक्त जा सकते थे ।
ना कोई इंटिमेशन
और नहीं कोई मैसेज देना पड़ता था,
बस यूँही उनसे मिलने चले जाते थे ।

कोई लौटा दे मेरे - वो बचपन के दिन।
जहां प्यार ही प्यार था, बहुत ही सिंपल लाइफ थी।

दिल्ली वालो क लिए –
अपना तो पहला प्यार, स्टूडेंट DTC बस पास था।
वो भी साढ़े बारह रुपया का था।
सिर्फ पॉकेट में बस पास होने पर,
लगता था दिल्ली सहर अपने जेब में है ।
दोस्तों के साथ मुक़ाबला होता था,
कौन सब से पहले बिना पेंसिल उठाये,
DTC लोगों बना सकता है ।

कोई लौटा दे मेरे - वो बचपन के दिन।
जहां प्यार ही प्यार था, बहुत ही सिंपल लाइफ थी।

गर्मियों में कुछ और ही मज़ा आता था छत पर सोने में ,
आसमान के नीचे बिस्तर लगाया करते थे।
टीमटीम करते सितारें और चंदा मामा
को देखते देखते आँखोमे नींद लाते थे।
कभी टूटता हुआ तारा देखते थे,
और विश मांगते थे।

कभी-कभी तो सप्तऋषि को ढून्ढ के,
ऊंगली से आसमान मे बनाते थे।

आंधी आने पर चद्दर से, अपने आप को ढककर रखते थे।
पर, बारिश आने से बिस्तर समेट कर,
भागके घरके अंदर होते थे।

कोई लौटा दे मेरे - वो बचपन के दिन।
जहां प्यार ही प्यार था, बहुत ही सिंपल लाइफ थी।

वो टाइम भी - क्या टाइम था,
दोस्तों के बिना जैसे जीवन अधूरा था।
तब हम कंही पर भी खेलते थे - रस्ते पर, ग्राउंड में, पार्क में
खेल ते, खेल ते सेतानी भी करते थे।
पड़ोसी के ग्लास विंडो तोड़के, फिर वंहा से भाग जाते थे।
और कभी पकड़े जाने पर, मुँह नहीं खोलते थे।

कोई लौटा दे मेरे - वो बचपन के दिन।
जहां प्यार ही प्यार था, बहुत ही सिंपल लाइफ थी।

अभी भी लगता है, यह सब कल की ही बातें है।
लाइफ सेटल के कम्पटीशन में,
कई दोस्त बहुत आगे निकल गए है।
और बाकि कुछ दोस्त थोड़ा पीछे रह गए है।
पर दोस्ती अपनी वही पुरानी वाली है।

कोई लौटा दे मेरे - वो बचपन के दिन।
जहां प्यार ही प्यार था, बहुत ही सिंपल लाइफ थी।

२२. एक कहानी

रात गुज़र गई।
सूरज की हल्की-हल्की,
किरणे कह रही है।

"जो गुज़र गया,
वह एक कहानी बन गई।
आज के लिए,
एक नया सादा पन्ना है।
कल वह भी,
एक कहानी होगी।

बस इतना ख़्याल रखना,
कहानी अधूरी ना छोड़ना।

हर एक दिन,
एक नई कहानी है।
जीवन -
जीवन एक उपन्यास है।

२३. ख़ुशी क्या है?

चलो, आज कुछ नया करते हैं,
"ख़ुशी" - जानने की कोशिश करते हैं।

दिन का शुरू सूरज से है,
चलो, सूरज से पूछते है - "ख़ुशी क्या है?"
सूरज ने कहा, "मेरे रोशनी से जब धरती जगमगाती है,
वही तो है ख़ुशी।"

आसमान में घूमते-घूमते,
बादल के पास पँहुचे,
बदल से पूछा - "ख़ुशी क्या है?"
बादल ने कहा, "जब धरती के लोग कड़क ते धूप से
परेशान होते है और मेरे आने से
उनको थोड़ी राहत मिलती है,
वही तो है ख़ुशी।"

बादल से बाहर आई तो बारिश होने लगी,
बारिश से पूछा - "ख़ुशी क्या है?"
बारिश ने कहा, "किसान जब मेरी ओर आस लगाएँ रहते हैं
और मैं उसी वक़्त बरसता हूँ,
तो उनके परेशानिया कम होती है,
वही तो है ख़ुशी।"

बारिश में भीगते-भीगते तारो के पास पहुँचे,
तारो से पूछा - "ख़ुशी क्या है?"
तारो ने कहा, "जब दो प्रेमी मेरे टिमटिमाती रौशनी में

मदहोश हो जाते है,
वही तो है खुशी।"

अंधेरे आसमान में एक चमकती रोशनी दिखाई दी,
पास जा कर देखा तो चांद नज़र आया।
चांद से पूछा - "ख़ुशी क्या है?"
चांद ने कहा, "जब माँ अपने रोते हुए बच्चे को दिखलाती है,
वह देखो चंदा मामा और वह बच्चा
मुस्कुराता है,
वही तो है खुशी।"

आसमान से ज़मीन पर आई, तो माँ मिली,
माँ से पूछा - "ख़ुशी क्या है?"
माँ ने कहा, "मेरे बच्चों का मुस्कुराता हुआ चेहरा,
वही तो है खुशी।"

सामने पिता बैठा था,
पिता से पूछा - "ख़ुशी क्या है?"
पिता ने कहा, "मेरे परिवार में कभी कोई कमी ना हो,
वही तो है खुशी।"

पास ही बेटा बैठा था,
बेटा से पूछा - "ख़ुशी क्या है?"
बेटे ने कहा, "मेरे वज़ह से मेरे माता पिता को
कभी सर ना झुकाना परे,
वही तो है खुशी।"

बेटी दौड़ी-दौड़ी आई,
बेटी से पूछा - "ख़ुशी क्या है?"
बेटी ने कहा, "मेरे वज़ह से कभी कोई तकलीफ ना हो,

हमेशा गर्व हो,
वही तो है खुशी।"

पीछे पति खड़ा था,
पति से पूछा - "ख़ुशी क्या है?"
पति ने कहा, "जब मैं घर लौटूं, पत्नी मेरी
मुस्कुराते हुए आलिंगन करे,
वही तो है खुशी।"

पत्नी चाय ले आई,
पत्नी से पूछा - "ख़ुशी क्या है?"
पत्नी ने कहा, "कभी कोई मुझे अवहेलना ना करे,
वही तो है खुशी।"

वँहा से निकले तो भाई मिला,
भाई से पूछा - "ख़ुशी क्या है?"
भाई ने कहा, "मेरी बहन के आँखों में कभी आँसू ना आये,
वही तो है खुशी।"

बहन पास बैठी थी,
बहन से पूछा- "ख़ुशी क्या है?"
बहन ने कहा, "मेरे भाई की तरक्की
वही तो है खुशी।"

घूमते घूमते दोस्त मिला,
दोस्त से पूछा - "ख़ुशी क्या है?"
दोस्त ने कहा, "अचानक बिछड़े दोस्त मिल जाते है,
वही तो है खुशी।"

सामने सखी दिखी,
सखी से पूछा - "ख़ुशी क्या है?"
सखी ने कहा, "साथ कभी ना छूटे,
वही तो है खुशी।"

चलते चलते मुसाफ़िर मिला,
मुसाफ़िर से पूछा - "ख़ुशी क्या है?"
मुसाफ़िर ने कहा, "मंजिल तक पहुँचना,
वही तो है खुशी।"

सामने देखा बगीचा,
बगीचे की हरियाली घास पर बैठे प्रेमी और प्रेमिका।
उनसे पूछा - "ख़ुशी क्या है?"
उन्होंने कहा,
"कभी हम जुदा ना हो,
वही तो है खुशी।"

बगीचे के सामने मंदिर
वंहा पुजारी मिला,
पुजारी से पूछा - "ख़ुशी क्या है?"
पुजारी ने कहा, "भगवान के दर पर विश्वास ले के आये हो,
वही तो है खुशी।"

किसको कितनी ख़ुशी मिली, ये कोई नहीं जानता।
पर,
"आपके चेहरे पर जो मुस्कान है,
वही तो ख़ुशी है।"

२४. कल मैं समा गया आज

कल में समा जाने वाली आज,
छोटी-छोटी ख़ुशियाँ दिये जा रहा है,
"समेट लो, समेट लो", मुस्कुरा के कह रहा है।

खुश रहने का पैगाम दे कर, आज का सुबह निकल गया।
खुश रहने का पैगाम दे कर, आज का सुबह निकल गया।

रात का इंतज़ार करते-करते शाम ढल रही है,
जाते-जाते, धीमे-धीमे कह रही है,
"दिल की बात कह डालो अभी,
ये पल, मिलेगा नहीं दोबारा कभी।"

कल में समा जाने वाली आज,
जाते-जाते कह रहा है,
"गम का परवाह मत करो,
तेज़ी से समय गुज़र रहा है।"

देखो-देखो, वो देखो,
कैसे, पल-पल समय निकल रहा है।
देखो-देखो, वो देखो,
00:00 बजे।
रात के बारह बज गया।
आज गुज़र गया,
कल मे समा गया।

Part 3

Fun with Colours in Canvas

A lonely Bird

Carona Mahakal

Rays of Hope

Snow Storm

Night View of Blossom

Mother's womb

Feel light like feather

Where to fly, dark on both sides

Night view of Niagara Falls in my colours

A rear piece of old carpet

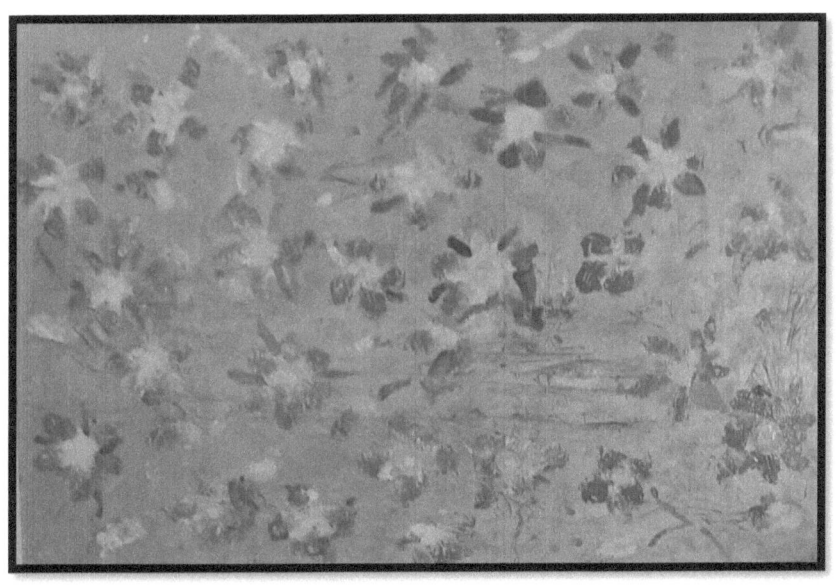

Arial view of scattered flowers

Blurred City view

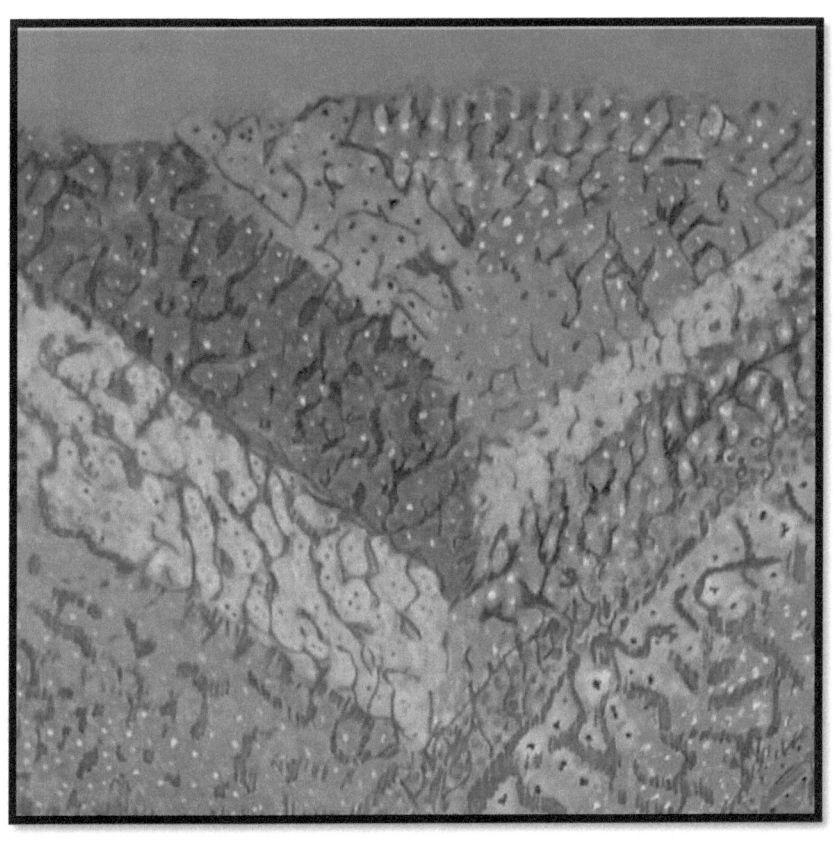

Valley of Flowers

Giant Honeycomb

Dancing Fountains (inside a cave)

Happy Hill

Colour Blast

Space view from my lens

Arrival of Spring

Deadly Storm

Falling Feathers

Milky Water Falls

Marble on canvas

Part 4

My first solo trip

Solo trip is a concept that fascinates many and helps you to explore oneself in a different way. I am also someone who always tries to do something new and loves to spread liveliness around unconditionally, so I opted for a solo trip as a medium.

It was morning around 9 am on 30th December 2022, I thought of a solo trip, although it was not planned, but I had a strong urge for it so I decided to experience and then Khajuraho, came in my mind, it is a place which I was longing to visit since long, and finally be my destination.

Deciding destination is not enough, you always have to make a lot of efforts that are the peripheral part of a journey, I also had to find train that directs me to my decided destination and then I booked my ticket, it was spontaneous and as my thoughts were flowing my actions were going accordingly, booking it on the same day, kept it on 'waiting' but, I was not bothered for it being not confirmed, rather I got busy with my daily works. Here, I noticed one thing: *when you have a firm decision, the outer unpleasant affairs lose their volume of intensity to bother you.*

Once, I got done with all my regular tasks, it was around 2.30 pm, I checked my phone and was surprised to see that my ticket got confirmed. Here, again I got to know that things happen when it has to happen, there is a famous dialogue in Hindi movie of Mr. Khan that **"Kehte hain agar kisi cheez ko dil se chaho to puri kainaat usse tumse milane ki koshish mein lag jaati hai"** (*If you love something with all your heart, then the whole universe tries to make you meet him.*).

Then I tried to book my return tickets immediately for 2nd Jan 2023. I booked my return ticket, it was also under 'waiting'. The very next thing was for a decent hotel for my stay. While exploring, I got to Khajuraho Inn, reviewed it, and contacted the concerned person at Khajuraho Inn to book a 2-day stay with the facilities of pick and drop. All booking formalities were completed by 4pm. Then I have started packing my clothes, preparing and packing some dinner as there is no pantry on the train. The train time was 6:33 pm, and it will halt for 2 mins at Nizamuddin station, New Delhi.

Finally, I left the house around 5:15 pm. Everything seems to be so quick that I failed to inform my daughter, who is always closest to my heart, and she is my motivator to such a decision to explore new places alone. When I was on the way to the station, I informed my daughter.

Honestly, informing is not that important but it plays an essential role with the people we are deeply associated with, because it makes others worry free.

Finally, I reached the station at 6.10 pm and boarded the train at the right time.

Aha, what a relief. It was such a hectic day.

I was joyful to get the window seat. My co-passengers were one couple and on the other side a mother with her daughter, all were traveling to Khajuraho.

After settling down, we started chatting with each other. While chatting with the couple, I came to know that the couple was from Kolkata, and they were speaking Hindi in Bengali tone. I am also a Bengali, so it's very easy for me to identify the Bengali in a crowd. Bengali is a sweet language but, it is little funny they speak it in "Hingali" (HaHa, I made this term), which means Hindi in Bengali tone.

The mother and daughter were from Noida.

In a very short time, we all became friendly to each other. And, that little girl offered us chips from her packet and at dinner time, we all had dinner together like a potluck — Bengali polao, dum aloo, matar puri, idlies with 2 types of chutney, gobi matar, chapati and some Bengali sweets. It was a delicious dinner. It was like a picnic on the train with so many varieties of food.

After dinner, we all planned to watch a movie on that little girl's laptop, but we were unable to hear the sound from her laptop, so I dropped the idea of watching a movie.

My fun trip started with the train journey itself.

As I was very tired, I started preparing my bed. We all were about to sleep but in our side berths, one gentleman started snoring sporadically. It was a terrible sound of snoring like falling some heavy metal from a height.

I could barely sleep in that night.

The next morning around 7 am, I reached my destination — Khajuraho.

My hotel cab was waiting outside the station before the scheduled time. I was looking for a coolie, but all the coolies were booked with others.

To come out from the station, I had to cross an over bridge with my luggage, but I found it a very difficult situation as 6 months back I had gone through a major operation and was not allowed to lift a weight.

So, I was looking for help as my cab driver was not entering the platform. Thankfully, two young boys around 24/25 years old helped me with my baggage to cross the bridge. The cab driver was at the gate, and he took the luggage from them and then to the cab.

Finally, I boarded the cab and reached the hotel within 15 mins.

After completing all formalities at the hotel reception, I entered my reserved room.

Without wasting any further time, I freshened up and had breakfast on the hotel terrace. While having breakfast, I decided to book a cab for the whole day for a city tour.

Following is some information about Khajuraho taken from Wikipedia.

In Khajuraho, out of 85 temples only 22 temples still exist. These temples are famous for their architecture and their sculptures. These have been divided into 3 Parts — Western group of temples, Southern group of temples and Eastern group of temples.

Western group of temples has a bigger area and more temples than the Southern and Eastern group of temples. Out of all these temples, one can worship only in one temple i.e. Matangeshwar temple — having a huge Shiva linga more than 6 ft. long and the rest of the idols are broken.

According to Hindu religious beliefs, if an idol is broken for some reason, it is not worshipped.

Following are the list of temples

Western Group of temples

- Chausath Yogini Temple
- Chitragupta temple
- Devi Jagadambi Temple
- Kandariya Mahadeva Temple
- Lakshmana Temple
- Lakshmi Temple
- Lalguan Mahadeva temple
- Matangeshwar Mahadeva Temple
- Nandi Temple
- Parvati Temple
- Varaha Temple
- Vishvanatha Temple

Eastern Group of temples :

Hindu :-

- Brahma Temple
- Javari Temple
- Vamana Temple

Jain temples :-

- Adinatha temple
- Parshvanatha temple
- Shantinatha temple
- Ghantai temple

Southern group temples

- Beejamandal
- Chaturbhuj Temple

The Light and Sound show is in Western Group of temples garden area.

Other than temples two more tourist points mesmerised me — **Kutni Island and Raneh Falls.**

I had another tourist attraction on my list, the Panna National Park, but due to time constraints, I was unable to book an entry ticket, so I dropped the idea of visiting Panna National Park and made a program for Orchha instead.

My day 1 city tour

The Western group of temples served as the starting point for my tour. I was told by my taxi driver that it would take around three hours to see the entire premises. The monuments are explained in detail by a guide who can be booked near the entrance.

In total, there are 12 temples, some big and some small. Every temple required climbing stairs, and each step was about 1 foot high. There is nothing uncomfortable about the temple floors; the stone releases my muscle sprains. I think it is only my own experience.

More glimpses about the temples can be found on the following pages.

After finishing the Western Group of temples, I was very hungry, and I was thinking of a decent restaurant for good food. Soon after leaving the gate, I became captivated by a board that displayed the address of Dada Boudir Hotel (Bengali food restaurant). Instead of looking for any other option, I called them and passed the call to my driver so he could locate them.

I reached the restaurant within 10 minutes. There, I ordered a Bengali mutton thali, since it was the last day of the year "mangsho bhaat to chai" (Mutton is a must on the last day of the year)

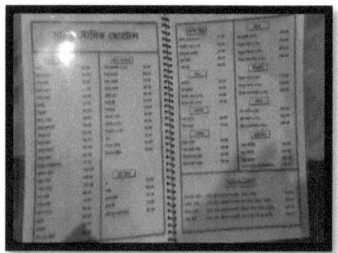 

I enjoyed a delicious meal before traveling to Kutni Island.

It is necessary to have an entry ticket in order to enter the island. Additionally, there is another counter inside the island for booking motor rides.

When I first arrived there, I was worried about taking a motor ride. A young couple was standing at the booking counter, looking for another person to book the entire boat. There was a norm that a boat could hold up to three people. I took my first-ever motor ride there.

Even though, I was a little more cautious about my movements after my operation. Honestly speaking, I enjoyed the ride fully as I had someone with me on the ride, giving me some relief.

Surprisingly, that day was the couple's 5th anniversary, and they also came for the first time to have some fun on a boat ride.

It wasn't in my fate that I would be able to stay long enough to see the sunset from that vantage point.

Since I wasn't wearing woollen and it was very cold, I decided to move out from that place. Moreover, my cab was also far from that place where I left my sweater and jacket.

Undoubtedly it was an aesthetic arrangement of nature, and I am blessed to preserve this stunning beauty in my memory.

From Kutni Island, I went to Raneh Waterfalls. Also known as the Grand Canyon of India. It has the most stunning beauty of nature, or you can call it one of the wonders of nature. It has a common entry point for Raneh Falls and the Ken Ghariyal Sanctuary. One needs to buy a ticket from the Madhya Pradesh Forest Dept. at the entrance, which also includes the guide fee.

The canyon is 5 km long into the path of the river Karnavati. It has a unique formation and the waterfalls are naturally formed while the canyons are shaped by under-earth volcanic eruptions a million years ago. These canyons are made of pure crystalline granite in varying shades of colours pink, red, black, yellow and brown. There are a series of waterfalls in the canyon. The larger and smaller falls run all through the year. During monsoon, the river Ken filled with water, covers most of this mini canyon and converts into a magnificent view of this place. My guide was telling me that during monsoon this place becomes 2nd Niagara Falls.

From there we drove further through the forest for 5 km where the river canyon opens up and there is a viewpoint from where one can see some crocodiles lying about 100 feet below, on the opposite river bank, and can be viewed through the guide's binoculars. The forest is mostly not dense and one can see antelopes, especially Nilgai, langurs, spotted deer and occasionally a fox. On my way, I could see deer, nilgai, chimpanzees, etc.

Overall, day 1 tour was amazing.

1. Western group of temples

2. Kutni Island

3. Raneh falls

Out of all these 3 breathtaking places, I like Raneh waterfalls the most. To gaze in wonder here we must look down to see the magical place because of under-earth volcanic eruptions.

My day 1 night program

While returning to the hotel after a day-long tour around 5:30 pm, I was very tired. But I craved New Year's Eve celebrations. I dropped the idea of going for a Light and Sound Show instead I asked the hotel owner to organise some light events at night to celebrate New Year's Eve. This hotel did not have any New Year's Eve celebrations. So, I requested them to organise a bonfire, music and just a cake. They agreed and arrangements were started. At night some couples came out of their room and others were preoccupied. Most of the people went out for drinks etc. But we had music, dance, a bonfire and cake in the hotel garden. So, the celebration of New Year's Eve and welcoming the new year 2023 by cake cutting were also fulfilled in my solo trip.

Around 1:30, the celebration got over, and we went back to our room to have a good night's sleep.

My day 2 city tour

The next morning, my program was to visit Orchha. When I woke up at 6 am, it was densely covered with fog, and it was very cold outside. So, I had to drop the idea of going to Orchha. The tour organiser said the distance from Khajuraho to Orchha is around 195 km, and it will take 3 hrs to drive to reach Orchha. Nevertheless, I took a rest and relaxed in my room at the hotel.

Around 11:30 am, the weather was better. So, I decided to visit the remaining part of Khajuraho i.e. Southern and Eastern Group of temples.

In the Southern group of temples, there are only 2 temples left to visit; the other temples were completely ruined.

First, I visited the "Chaturbhuja" temple which means "One who has four arms" which is an epithet of Vishnu. The temple was built by Yasovarman of the Chandela Dynasty. This is the only temple in Khajuraho which lacks erotic sculptures.

Chaturbhuja

Thereafter, I visited the Duladeo Temple.

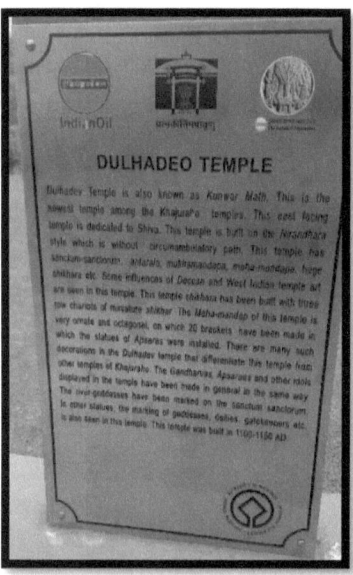

The temple is dedicated to the god Shiva in the form of a linga, which is deified in the sanctum. 'Duladeo' means "Holy Bridegroom". The temple is also known as "Kunwar Math". The temple faces east was built during 1100-1150 AD. It is the last of the temples built during the Chandela period. The temple is laid in the seven-chariot plan (saptaratna). The figurines carved in the temple have soft expressive features unlike other temples. The walls have a display of carved celestial dancers (apsara) in erotic postures and other figures.

From there I went to visit the Eastern group of temples. In this whole compound, one can see temples of Hindu, Jain and Buddhist.

The following information is taken from Wikipedia.

Parsvanatha temple built between 950 AD and 970 AD is the biggest temple in the Eastern cluster. This temple is said to be designed by the master Dhangadeva and was initially dedicated to the first Jain Tirthankara, Adinatha. In 1860, the statue of Adinatha was removed and the current one of Parsavnatha was installed and has been known as the Parsvanatha temple since then. This temple is different from the other temples in Khajuraho, where this one is built at a low plinth level as against the high platforms of the other temples, making it easier for visitors to view the sculptures at closer quarters.

Adinath Temple - This temple is located to the north of the Parsvanatha temple. This temple is in a state of disrepair and only the sanctum and the entrance hall exist today. Adinath temple is known for the splendid sculptures involving a string of musicians playing various instruments and sensuous sculptures of dancing apsaras.

Brahma Temple - Located on the banks of Ninora- Tal, this temple has a Shikara made of sandstone and a body made of granite. This temple, though called the Brahma temple, is touted to be dedicated to Lord Vishnu who embraces the major wall of the temple. The temple is simple in plan and execution and consists of a pyramidal Shikara crowned by a prominent bell tower-like structure.

Ghantai Temple - This temple is named after the chain and bell motifs (Ghanta), which are inscribed into the pillars of this temple. The temple was conceived in much larger proportions than the Parsvanatha temple, but today only the Mahamandap and entrance porch supported by four tall pillars exist. The coffered ceiling of the entrance porch is covered with exquisite images of dancers and musicians. The door of the temple bears the figure of an eight-armed yakshi Chakresvari, seated on a garuda. The external wall of the temple has sculptures of the sixteen signs that the mother of the holy Jina Mahavira, saw in the dream during conception.

Vamana and Javeri Temple - Javeri temple is dedicated to Lord Vishnu and exhibits one of the most delicate architectures among all the temples here. This temple is named after the Jawari millet which grows in this region. It was built between 1075 and 1100 AD. This temple is especially known for the exquisite Makara torana motifs and the soaring Shikara. Another famous Vamana temple dates back to between 1050 and 1075 AD and is dedicated to one of the ten avatars of Lord Vishnu, the Vamana avatar. This temple is conspicuous amongst the temples in Khajuraho by the absence of erotic sculptures except in the niches in the pediments. This absence of any erotic or sensual figures indicates that this temple is later than the Kandariya

Mahadev temple though it follows the architectural style and sculptural types.

Hanuman Statue in Khajuraho This colossal statue of Lord Hanuman is located in a comparatively modern structure halfway between the western cluster and the Khajuraho village. This temple is interesting mainly because of the dedicatory inscription on its pedestal dated the year 316, possibly belonging to the Harsha era (922AD), being the oldest dated inscription at the place.

Eastern group of temples - Finest Art and Sculpture temples

After completing the Southern and Eastern group of temples tour, around 2 pm, I had a very simple lunch (maach bhaat thali — fish and rice) at the same Dada Boudir hotel.

Thereafter, I was back at the hotel by 3 pm.

Since I missed the sunset on Kutni Island and could not visit the same again due to the shortage of time. Around 4 pm, I decided to see the first sunset of the year 2023 in Beni Sagar Dam which was 5 km away from my hotel. There I had a good fun time with the sun and did some sunset photography. That evening, I named it a **"Fun with Sun"**.

139 | The Dawn of Life: Supernova Innings

My day 2 Night program

Thereafter, my driver dropped me at Western group of temples to visit Matangeshwar temple and for the Light and Sound show.

Matangeshwar temple — It is located amongst the Western group of temples. Amongst the Chandela-era monuments of Khajuraho, it is the only Hindu temple that is still actively used for worship. It is not richly decorated: its interior walls, exterior walls and curvilinear tower are devoid of carving.

Since it was the first day of the year, the temple was heavily crowded to visit and worship. I couldn't be in that crowd. So, I left that place, and instead, I explored the market till the ticket counter opened for the Light and Sound show.

There are two shows one will begin at 6:30 pm English and Hindi will begin at 7:30 pm. The 6:30 pm show appealed to me since I was there from 5:30 pm.

Meanwhile, I had tea and bought a pack full of freshly roasted whole peanuts which I kept in my pocket keeping in mind that during the show I will have that one by one. Back to the ticket counter and bought a ticket for an English show.

The garden premise was huge and chairs were lined up. There were no reserved seats, so anyone could sit anywhere.

I chose a corner seat.

After a long time, I could see the wide night sky. The sky was clear and charming to see twinkling stars and the moon, though it was not a full moon.

The weather was also very pleasant.

The show began at 6:30 pm. While going through the show, I had peanuts in the open air under moonlight and stars. I was so emotional at that moment tears came out as I felt like I had gone back to my childhood. I used to have these peanuts in the Durga puja pandal at the time of evening cultural programs or Bengali movies on a cloth screen with projector and film reels.

In our childhood, we watched Bengali movies only on the Durga puja pandal. All these childhood memories came alive.

After many years, I saw the Light and Sound show that too in Khajuraho. It was a splendid show.

After the show, once again I visited the Matangeshwar shrine around 8 pm. At that time the temple was empty. I could easily enter the temple and see the huge Shiva Linga closely. The height of the Shiva Linga is about 2.5 meters. I have never seen such a big Shiva Linga before. The size of the Linga is more than an average man's height.

Also, I could see a Ganesha statue at the entrance.

Thereafter, I went to a decent roadside Dhaba for dinner. To celebrate the first dinner of the year 2023, I ordered Mutton Rogan Josh, garlic naan with salad and raita.

From there I returned straight to the hotel around 10 pm. At that time, there were very few vehicles on the road and very few people were roaming around. There was a sense of silence at midnight.

Day 3 — Orchha

The next day at 3:30 in the morning I woke up, and I didn't sleep well at night. It was my last day in Khajuraho, and I had planned to travel to Orchha at 7am. However, the cab driver did not pick up my calls. His phone was switched off.

To find an alternative solution, I contacted the property owner and raised the issue with him. The driver was also not responsive when he tried to contact him. Consequently, he had to arrange a new cab and it arrived at 7:45 p.m.

Although it was not foggy, it was cloudy and cold.

The road and the highway were vehicle-free at that time. The driver drove at a speed of 60km per hour. On the highway, we can't imagine travelling at this speed.

Finally, I arrived at Orchha around 11am.

My driver took me first to Sheesh Mahal, which is flanked on either side by the Raja Mahal and the Jahangir Mahal. This has royal accommodation, which was built for King Udait Singh. It has now been converted into a hotel with suites on the upper floor. There is also a large hall with high ceiling, which is the dining hall.

I was extremely hungry because I had not eaten breakfast. To begin my visit, I ordered breakfast at Sheesh Mahal, which has now been converted into a restaurant.

After ordering puri sabji, I proceeded to freshen up.

Their washroom was upstairs next to the terrace, so I walked up to the terrace and took pictures of the surroundings. But the funny part was that the restaurant man was looking for me as breakfast was ready, and it was served at my table. He came upstairs and looked for me. Finally, when he saw me on the terrace taking pictures, he scolded me.

Then I came down and had a filling breakfast as the Orchha tour will take another 4hrs.

I started my tour from the fort complex, one side is Jahangir Mahal and the other side is Raja Mahal, and in between is Sheesh Mahal, where I had my breakfast.

Information from Wikipedia :

The fort and other structures within it were built by the Bundela Rajputs starting in the early 16th century by King Rudra Pratap Singh of the Orchha State and others who followed him. The fort complex, which is accessed from an arched causeway, leads to a large gateway. This is followed by a large quadrangular open yard surrounded by palaces. These are the Raja Mahal, Sheesh Mahal, Jahangir Mahal, a temple, gardens and pavilions. The battlements of the fort have ornamentation. Notable architectural features in the fort complex are projecting balconies, open flat areas and decorated latticed windows.

First, I went to Jahangir Palace.

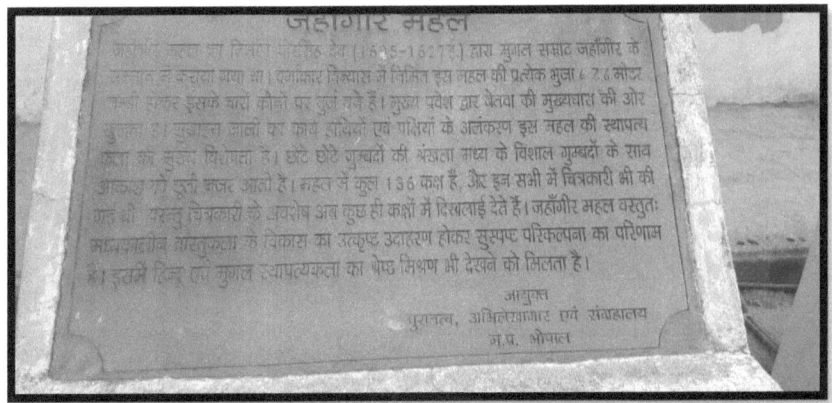

*Jahangir Palace – more glimpses on following pages

Jahangir Mahal is a palace that was exclusively built by Bir Singh Deo in 1605 for the Mugal emperor Jahangir who was a guest of the Maharaja for one night only. The palace is built in four levels with architectural features of both Muslim and Rajput architecture. Its layout is a symmetrical square, built in the inner courtyard of the fort, and has eight large domes. The roof above the top floor of this Mahal is accessed through a steep stairway. It provides views of the temples and the Betwa River outside the fort complex. The palace also houses a small archaeological museum.

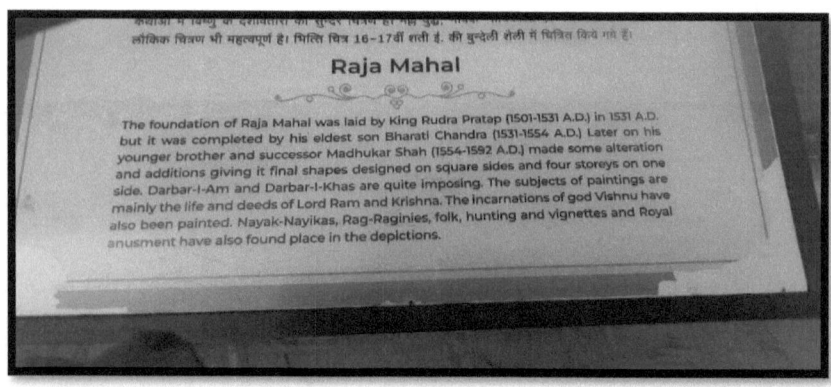

** Raja Mahal – more pictures on following pages

The Raja Mahal (King's Palace), where the kings and the queens had resided till it was abandoned in 1783, was built in the early part of 16th century. Its exterior is simple and unembellished, but the interior chambers of the palace are elaborately royal in their architectural design, decorated with murals of social and religious themes of gods, mythical animals, and people. In the upper floor of the palace, there are traces of mirrors in the ceilings and walls. Its windows, arcaded passages, and layout plan are designed in such a way that the "sunlight and shadow create areas of different moods and temperatures throughout the day". The interior walls of the Mahal have murals of Lord Vishnu. The Mahal has several secret passages.

From Raja Mahal, I went to Chaturbhuj Temple. It took only 5 minute drive from Raja Mahal.

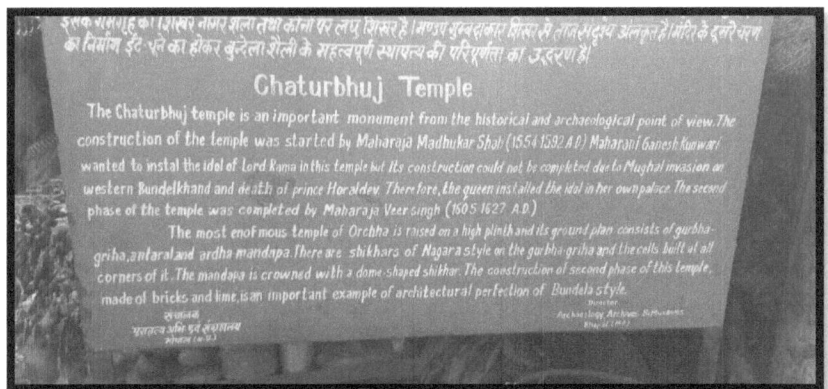

The Chaturbhuj temple has tall spires in the shape of pine cones built atop a high platform of 4.5 metres (15 ft) height. The overall height of the temple is 105 metres (344 ft). The imposing view of the temple is that of multi-storied palace with arcaded openings, a very large entrance, a large central tower and fortifications. The climb to the temple facade involves climbing steep and narrow steps numbering 67, which forming a winding stairway.

At present an image of Radha Krishna is worshipped in Chaturbhuj Temple.

Ram Raja Mandir

Ram Raja Mandir is located next to Chaturbhuj temple. As there was a long line to enter Ram Mandir, and since I had a limited amount of time, I did not enter the temple and I moved directly to Chaturbhuj temple.

And I took this picture from Chaturbhuj temple before leaving the premises.

Information about Ram Raja Mandir taken from Wikipedia.

In India this is the only temple where God Rama is worshiped as a king and that too in a palace. A Guard of Honour is held every day, police personnel have been designated as Guards at the temple, much in the manner of a king. The food and other amenities provided to the deity at the temple are a royal repast. Armed salutation is provided to God Ram every day.

The speciality of this temple is that God Ram has a sword in his right hand and a shield in the other. Shri Ram is sitting in Padmasan, with the left leg crossed over the right thigh.

Betwa River, Orchha

After visiting all the three main tourist spots in Orchha, my driver took me to the Betwa River side while returning to the hotel. That was a fleeting visit as I was running short of time.

People usually go rafting there and it is a scenic site with the fort's boundary wall visible from there. I took some pictures and enjoyed the riverside on the rocks. I could barely spend 10 to 15 minutes there. I could spend more time there but I had to return to the hotel by 5 pm to catch my train around 6 pm.

A sweet memory in the yellow field, on the way back Orchha

I enjoyed observing yellow fields along both sides of the highway during my drive from Khajuraho to Orchha and again upon returning from Orchha. Due to my inability to control my emotions, I asked the driver to stop somewhere near the field, so that, I could take some pictures of these beautiful fields.

The driver told me he would stop where I could get into the field. All fields are fenced with wire and gated as well. He stopped in one of the fields, but I could not enter it as the road towards the field was a sharp slope. I tried, but it was too slippery so I dropped the idea. But my driver said he would take me to another field.

A further 15 minutes of driving later, he stopped the cab near another field. In that field, I met Shivani, a class 8 student. In addition to showing me the fields on both sides of the highway, she assisted me with getting into one of their fields. It was a pleasure to spend time with her in yellow field. She was my photographer at that time. Also, she was enjoying taking my pictures. I shared my shades and cap with her and captured some pictures for memories. Interestingly, she posed and removed her dupatta while I was taking her pictures. We both had a great time in the yellow field.

It was a real fun time with her. I would like to reciprocate this gesture by providing her with a token of love. However, there was only one packet of Little Hearts in my bag, so I gave it to a very sweet little one.

My photographers during my trip

1. Random tourists
2. Locals
3. My driver
4. My guide
5. Security guard
6. Myself

My driver

Sweet little girl

Security guard

Guide

The story behind Khajuraho Inn

The day my Orchha trip was cancelled, I sat at the reception and other residents were also there. We all chatted about life. During our conversation, one of them said I looked like 44 years old. That was the biggest compliment I got on the first day of 2023.

After some time, the property owner also joined us. While chatting with him, I learned more about his life.

His name is Gautam Vijay. He belongs to a Khajuraho Brahman family. His entire family is involved in temples as pandits. He always wanted to do something different though he knew all the rituals and mantras of pujas. Instead of becoming a pandit at temples, he graduated in Chinese language from Taiwan University. In addition, he travelled to Japan and other countries to learn more languages.

At the age of 25, he lost his father and returned home. Since he is the eldest son, he has to look after his entire family. He has 2 sisters and 1 brother. Both sisters are married now.

He organised India tours for foreigners and worked in hotels. However, he was dissatisfied with his work. In the course of his career, he had always dreamed of owning his own hotel. Having worked in hotels for many years, he eventually opened Khajuraho Inn in March 2017.

He is gentle, polite and down to earth. Always ready to help his guests whenever they need it.

When he found out that I am a 58 years old lady and a solo traveller, out of respect he organised my whole tour. And when I left the hotel, he dropped me at the station and helped me board the train with my luggage. A minute before the train started, he brought a bottle of water for me and wished me to come again. The hospitality was excellent.

The last sentence he said to me was, "Umeed mein duniya tiki hai" (the world lives on in hopes).

Lesson on divine path

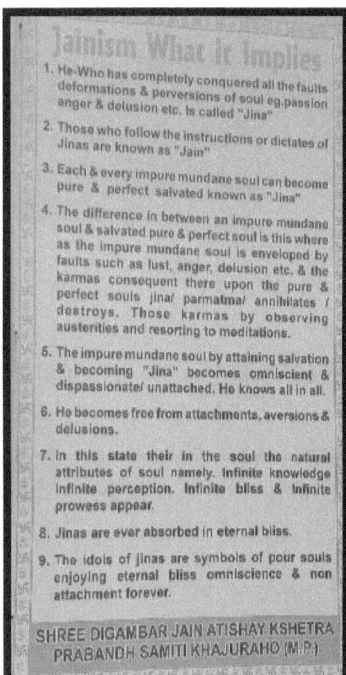

Jainism What it Implies

1. He-Who has completely conquered all the faults deformations & perversions of soul eg.passion anger & delusion etc. Is called "Jina"

2. Those who follow the instructions or dictates of Jinas are known as "Jain"

3. Each & every impure mundane soul can become pure & perfect salvated known as "Jina"

4. The difference in between an impure mundane soul & salvated pure & perfect soul is this where as the impure mundane soul is enveloped by faults such as lust, anger, delusion etc. & the karmas consequent there upon the pure & perfect souls jina/ parmatma/ annihilates / destroys. Those karmas by observing austerities and resorting to meditations.

5. The impure mundane soul by attaining salvation & becoming "Jina" becomes omniscient & dispassionate/ unattached. He knows all in all.

6. He becomes free from attachments, aversions & delusions.

7. In this state their in the soul the natural attributes of soul namely. Infinite knowledge Infinite perception. Infinite bliss & Infinite prowess appear.

8. Jinas are ever absorbed in eternal bliss.

9. The idols of jinas are symbols of pour souls enjoying eternal bliss omniscience & non attachment forever.

SHREE DIGAMBAR JAIN ATISHAY KSHETRA
PRABANDH SAMITI KHAJURAHO (M.P.)

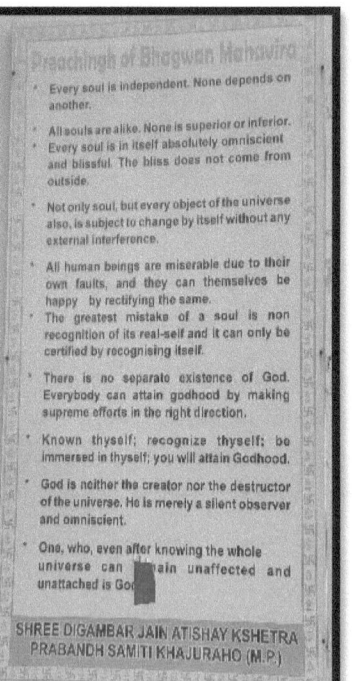

Preachingh of Bhagwan Mahavira

- Every soul is independent. None depends on another.
- All souls are alike. None is superior or inferior.
- Every soul is in itself absolutely omniscient and blissful. The bliss does not come from outside.
- Not only soul, but every object of the universe also, is subject to change by itself without any external interference.
- All human beings are miserable due to their own faults, and they can themselves be happy by rectifying the same.
- The greatest mistake of a soul is non recognition of its real-self and it can only be certified by recognising itself.
- There is no separate existence of God. Everybody can attain godhood by making supreme efforts in the right direction.
- Known thyself; recognize thyself; be immersed in thyself; you will attain Godhood.
- God is neither the creator nor the destructor of the universe. He is merely a silent observer and omniscient.
- One, who, even after knowing the whole universe can remain unaffected and unattached is God

SHREE DIGAMBAR JAIN ATISHAY KSHETRA
PRABANDH SAMITI KHAJURAHO (M.P.)

The End of my first solo trip

During my return journey, I thought about my entire trip. The experience was fun and filled with fond memories.

As a result of my first-ever unplanned solo trip, I am incredibly satisfied and confident that I will continue to travel on my own in the future.

I reached Nizamuddin Station, New Delhi at 8 am on 3rd Jan 2023 and finally made it home with so many happy memories.

As a whole, my first solo trip was my soul trip as well.

Upon returning from my solo trip, I was so inspired by so many beautiful sculptures that these lines popped into my head.

"बिन पिए नशा का जादू, कुछ और ही हैं;

पीने वालो का नशा, तो एक आदत हैं;

बेजुबान मूर्ति का नशा, इश्क़ होने का ख़तरा हैं"

Without alcohol, intoxication is a different phenomenon;

Drinking intoxicates, and becoming addicted to it is a habit;

The risk of intoxication with a speechless idol is the risk of falling in love.

Some more glimpses of my solo trip

Western group of temple area

Jahangir Palace

Raja Mahal

Distorted paintings inside Raja Mahal

Chaturbhuja Temple

Some close photography of sculptures

Before you step up in any temple, you will see this. Similar to a doormat before entering a house, it appears to clean footwear and prevent dirt from entering temples.

There is a common structure throughout all temples on top of each pillar for holding the ceiling, Lord Virel (Kichak).

In this image, a lion is portrayed as a symbol of Raja and a child is portrayed as a symbol of obstacles. The lion grasping the child symbolizes the king's ability to overcome all obstacles.

There is only one statue of Lakshmi Ganesha in the entire premises of art and sculpture at Khajuraho.

This unique idol shows 3 Hindu gods. Shiva is portrayed on top with Vishnu in the middle and Krishna from the waist down to his cross legs and feet. It is the only idol inside the Chaturbhuja temple, Khajuraho

The erotic sculptures can be seen in the middle column.

Half of the idol represents Shiva, and the other half represents Parvati.

Some glimpses of broken idols inside Western group of temples

Some Random Pictures During My Solo Trip

www.ingramcontent.com/pod-product-compliance
Lightning Source LLC
LaVergne TN
LVHW041939070526
838199LV00051BA/2838